Almost Brown

Almost Brown

A MEMOIR

Charlotte Gill

CROWN
NEW YORK

Published in the United States by Crown, an imprint of Random House, a division of Penguin Random House LLC, New York.

CROWN and the Crown colophon are registered trademarks of Penguin Random House LLC.

Hardback ISBN 978-0-593-44301-9
Ebook ISBN 978-0-593-44302-6

PRINTED IN CANADA ON ACID-FREE PAPER

crownpublishing.com

2 4 6 8 9 7 5 3 1

First Edition

For my dad

In general, mixed bloods are considered to be intermediate in physical and cultural traits and to have intermediary roles. This generalization requires some qualification.

—Everett V. Stonequist, *The Marginal Man*

CONTENTS

Part 1

Part 2

PART

A LITTLE 1 CIRCLE

MY FATHER'S SKIN IS THE COLOR OF A MEDIUM-roasted coffee bean. His eyes are so dark you can't tell the pupils from the irises. His hair was once nearly black, but now it's white—at least it is when he doesn't get around to coloring it. He disguises his gray from time to time at a salon he's been visiting for at least a couple of decades. We probably share the same dye shade—*espresso brown,* according to my drugstore box.

He has half-moons of darker pigmentation beneath his eyes, which are slightly puffy about the upper lids and slightly downturned at the outer corners. Many of us in the family share this trait, and if we aren't smiling in photos, we tend to look sleepy, sad, or both, even if we're having the best time. My dad has a pleasingly round face, also a common family feature, inherited from my grandmother. His family is Sikh, although he isn't what I'd call religious. And neither am I, which pleases him immensely, especially since my mother has become more churchgoing with time. In this way, if not elsewhere, I'm a fulfillment of his design.

He was born in Punjab, India, and has lived on four continents, but somehow he ended up in South Texas. He lives in McAllen, a city known for its Customs and Border Patrol detention facilities and gargantuan public library fashioned from an abandoned Walmart. Wherever he goes, people still call him "Dr. Gill." Once a physician, always a physician.

He's also an Anglophile. For years, he lived in the United Kingdom. It's where he trained to be a surgeon. He still loves marmalade and orange pekoe tea and table manners and the Queen's English and generally most kinds of fusty British pomp except the royal family, whom he quietly dislikes. He sprinkles his sentences with "bloody well" and "bloody hell" when he's grumpy. He still defends Great Britain as the height of civilized achievement, which I sometimes think is a form of internalized prejudice.

For a man born in the Hindenburg era, he's impressively adept with technology. He owns the latest iPhone, and his ringtone is bonging church bells—a strange choice for a Sikh person, one of his many fascinating contradictions. When his phone rings, he wrangles it out of his pocket, glances down at the screen, and usually decides to ignore it, at least when I'm around. He's a competent driver with no plans to give up his license, at least not without a fight. He wore glasses from middle age until just recently, when he had his cataracts removed and his vision corrected with laser surgery. He has good white teeth, mostly his own, which have always been the animating feature of his face when he smiles. He can go from looking hard and brooding to effervescently playful in an eyeblink.

My father is an eighty-six-year-old who has now spent more time as a bachelor than he ever did a married man. He celebrated his eightieth birthday twice; the first time he forgot he was only seventy-nine. Or he claims he forgot. No one loves the twinkle of a good party like he does, except maybe me, if the moment is right.

MY DAD SHUFFLES into the living room wearing his voluminous bathrobe. He says he had a wretched sleep, that's why he woke up so late, even though I know perfectly well what time he returned last night from his favorite bar and can guess how many Bollywood movies he started into before dawn.

"What time did you get back?" I ask, the kind of question he might have had for me back in my days of youthful mayhem.

"Oh," he says, "not too late," which is the type of shady reply I would have given back then also.

He bumps his way between the coffee table and the sofa, then eases himself down. He rummages for the TV remote among the cushions while reminding me of his virtuously early mornings back when he still worked in hospitals. Our memories diverge on this and other things, but I don't mention it.

I'm slouched across the love seat with my laptop open. He sits in the middle of the big sofa. He flicks on the giant flat-screen TV, and we watch together for a while. Often, it's some aristocratically slow sporting event like cricket or golf. Either that or the news. My dad likes the unfettered punditry of American broadcast journalism, the more inflamed the propaganda the better. The TV is his campfire, a loud one, even though he can still hear perfectly well.

Lazy afternoon light beams through the living room windows. I hear the letter carrier shove the mail through the slot, and then it lands heavily on the foyer floor. My dad channel surfs at dizzying speeds. His TV pumps out almost every satellite signal transmitted between space and the earth. We skip over ads for pharmaceuticals featuring actors enjoying their vitality and ads for ambulance-chasing lawyers engaged in class-action suits. It's as if he's looking for something rare and particular that is nowhere to be found.

I say, "Wouldn't it be better for your biorhythms or whatever to go to bed, you know, at a more normal human hour?" It's a refrain he hears often from other well-meaning relatives, all our comments about his upside-down schedule.

My dad's face contracts into a scowl. He waves at the air between us to express his opinion about my attitude. I've seen this gesture a thousand times over the years, and I still can't decide if he's doing it for his relief or my entertainment—maybe a little of both. I love it when he acts as if I'm driving him around the bend. I laugh, he shakes his head, and then we go back to surfing together.

A LITTLE LATER, he disappears into his bedroom, and then he emerges wearing beige medical scrubs. He owns many sets in several colors, and he often wears them to his physical therapy appointments as ersatz athletic apparel, since he owns no articles of gym clothing, at least none that were made in this century.

"I don't think brown looks good on me," he says.

"It doesn't look good on me, either," I reply.

He sinks down on the sofa to apply sneakers to feet. He used to have an impressive collection of well-made leather shoes, but podiatric troubles have reduced him to a single pair of slide-ons that give him a kind of accidental gentleman-hipster cool. He puts these on with a long shoehorn he keeps beneath the coffee table. Then he takes his blood pressure. The wrist cuff beeps and deflates.

"Do you want me to drive you?"

"No, no," he says, frowning, swatting me away. "Don't worry about it." He's been going to therapy to work on his leg strength lately. Mobility and independence go hand in hand—this reality isn't lost on him. One wipeout in the shower, and that's it, the end of his ability to live as he pleases. But he never lets me anywhere near the clinic, not even to run errands in the neighborhood while he's inside.

Now he's running late, as always, I can tell from his tone, and the prospect of my company is just another obstacle that threatens to slow him down. He pockets his iPhone and keys then shuffles out through the kitchen to the garage, where I hear the door lift and his car engine cough to life. Normally, if there's an appointment with the dentist or the rheumatologist that he'd rather avoid, he'll blow it off. My semi-informed guess is that his therapist is an attractive, attentive woman upon whom he has a mild crush.

MY DAD OWNS a modest unit in a brick-and-terra-cotta subdivision—an atypical surgeon's retirement—with news-papers piled up on the doorstep and at least a few of the lightbulbs burned out. His house was built in the eighties and hardly anything has been renovated since then. There's an atrium painted pistachio green. The bathrooms, mine and his, feature gold taps with clear acrylic knobs cut to resemble diamonds.

I wait until he's gone to tidy up, otherwise he tells me not to do it, but only half-heartedly. I start in the living room, which is the biggest enigma, a bafflement of fatherly detritus. He spends plenty of time in here, and it has accumulated a snow of his belongings, none of which seems to have proper stowage.

The glass coffee table is covered on the westerly end with a library of orange prescription bottles and Ayurvedic remedies sent to him in the mail by his sisters. A lot of it is expired or untouched, but still, he won't allow me to dispose of any of these, as if it is a little shrine to his personal medical adventures. On the other end, there is a rampart of magazines, a medical journal or two, and sometimes the odd book that he says I should read, but that he has not read himself. In between there is evidence of snacking—a paper towel stained with a cup ring, a plate with a few flakes of samosa pastry, and a tiny plastic pot of tamarind chutney. Usually there's a bowl of Lindor chocolates somewhere in this vicinity, even though he's the only person I know in the world who doesn't like chocolate. I wonder who it's there for—maybe me.

My father dislikes most vegetables but loves fruit. I find the evidence of his midnight snacking, skins and peelings set down on many of the horizontal surfaces. He has a supertaster palate. He swears he can detect the residue, in a cup of orange pekoe, of tea bag paper. He will order two single espressos at once because, according to him, they're superior to one double shot. He doesn't like chicken. He says it's "tasteless" due to modern factory farming methods, but once when he was visiting me, I fed him a slow-roasted organic hen who'd lived a happy, pastoral life courtesy of a farmer named Matt. He didn't like that, either. He's also very sensitive to smells. He will walk into a space and detect any noxious aroma, no matter how infinitesimally molecular, and declare that the room has "a pong."

Right by the front door, in a decorating vignette with terrible chi, my dad keeps a small writing desk with an old inkjet printer and an even more ancient laptop that's as heavy as a paving stone. Its drawers are empty save various info sheets left behind by the internet- and cable-installation guys who frequent the house when things go technically awry or when he forgets his wifi password. Also near the door, an old treadmill gathers dust. He says he uses it, but I've yet to see this with my own eyes. More confounding still is the wheeled trolley that houses a junk-drawer assortment of things that have washed in via the front door: kaput medical contraptions, window-cleaning flyers, more self-prescribed medications delivered in stapled paper bags.

In the corner there's a recliner where he sits with his feet up from time to time when he's not at his mission control on the couch, a type of furniture he referred to in my childhood as "a settee." The sofas are white leather, oversized and very soft to the touch, and when you sit in them it's like sinking into a marshmallow. At the opposite end of the design spectrum, my dad's house features a lot of dark timber, a style reminiscent of the British colonial era. In particular I'm thinking of the floor, which looks like it might have been crafted from some kind of endangered hardwood.

My dad's bookcase carries few books. He says he doesn't have the visual stamina to read for long periods anymore. Unlike other Indian dads, his favorite pastimes aren't chai and the gurdwara but other, more decadent attractions. In the shelves, he keeps an unused tea set, a JFK commemorative plate, and a bottle of Louis XIII cognac, displayed in a

satin clamshell box but never consumed. There are framed
snapshots that others have given him, capturing the high
points in their mutual social lives. Some of these people I've
met, and some I haven't. One wall is reserved for childhood
photos of us, his kids, most of them taken by our mother,
who was always the camera buff. She doesn't appear in this
rogues' gallery, except for one awkwardly reassembled family photo taken at my brother's wedding. My dad doesn't
take photos much at all. He lives in the moment.

Next, I change the sheets on his bed, a massive sleigh,
also made of dark wood, with a high, king-sized mattress. In
the sheets, I find evidence of his horizontal nibbling in the
form of a flattened, partially eaten muffin, and I wonder
when and where exactly he picked up this baked good. He
tells me often that he doesn't sleep well anymore, never
through the whole night. He has another giant flat screen in
his bedroom. In the small hours, in addition to his Bollywood explorations, he watches old classic movies like *The
Bridge on the River Kwai* or basically anything starring
Peter O'Toole. In his contemporary tastes, he gravitates
toward storylines with underdog geniuses who struggle for
basic recognition in an unfair world: *The Man Who Knew
Infinity* or *Hidden Figures*. I know a lot about his cinematic
tendencies because I once loaned him my password for "the
Netflix," as he calls it. During this period, he cycled through
such a vast array of partially watched Bollywood films that
my husband made me cut him off for "screwing up our algorithm," in the process swamping both our landing pages
with Hindi blockbusters.

In his darkened cave, I push back the curtains and fold
the laundry. The master bedroom has a large en suite that's
less like a bathroom and more like the dressing room of a

warhorse theater actor. There's a broad vanity, a sink made to look like gold-veined marble, and a big mirror before a large walk-in closet, which is fitting, since my dad loves clothes.

My cousins call him, with a certain affectionate irony, "Silk Singh." I don't live with my dad or anywhere close by. I reside in a small Canadian town where a common men's uniform is Carhartts utility pants, a logger's sweater, and a ball cap with sunglasses perched on the brim. The last time my father came to visit me, he got off the plane wearing a pink shirt and a cream-colored suit with a magenta pocket square, looking like Tom Wolfe at his most sartorially florid, if Tom Wolfe was a brown guy with a penchant for gold jewelry.

He no longer wears a turban, a kirpan, a steel bangle, or any other of the ceremonial signs of initiated Sikhdom—by choice and necessity. My father is now a Western man. He's proud to be an American citizen. Not a landed immigrant, not a legal alien—an American. He has been known to wear a fedora and an ascot at the same time, a style I might describe as Hunter S. Thompson meets Willy Wonka, with a nod, in his more casual moments, to polo and safari themes. He often wears a gold Rolex. It's probably real, but I can't say for sure.

My dad's closet is like a very small museum devoted to his personal fashion history over the decades. The shelves are stacked with cashmere turtlenecks and cable-knit sweaters with leather buttons, seldom worn at this subtropical latitude. He owns over a hundred ties in every color, most of them silk, surpassed only by his collection of collared shirts. I've never counted, but they must run well into the hundreds. He claims to have twenty suits, although I suspect there are more tucked away in his various household closets, along with several blazers, some in velvet, some with brass buttons. When we lived in more northern climes he wore tailored wool suits, sometimes three-piece versions, to work every day, and they must be here, too, lurking around at the back, sheathed in plastic.

He used to own an Imelda Marcos–sized trove of shoes, not oxfords or brogues, but mostly loafers in horse-bit, full-strap, tassel, and monk-strap form, many of which still sit in his closet today, the leather stiff with disuse, along with a pair of white eighties-vintage Reeboks in perfectly preserved condition. I find at least a few pieces of outerwear, raincoats and parkas embroidered with the names of the tourist towns and cruise ship ports where he bought them, compelled in the moment by a downpour or an unforeseen cold snap. My dad is not a fan of heavy weather, nor its power to devastate a fashion look in seconds. Not too cold and not too hot is the perfect state of affairs.

You can tell at a glance what catches his eye at the retail racks: silky fabrics and sumptuous textures, but also, in contrast, mercilessly starched cotton. He's a magpie, attracted by shiny objects and effulgent colors, and in a world of beiges, whites, and grays, what's so bad about that? A peek in his closet reveals a thousand articles, a thousand votes for the transformative powers of clothing, its ability to lift the wearer from one station or mood to another one higher up. He's not fastidious about his creases, either. It's simply a pleasure. For my dad, dressing well and for the occasion is also a sign of bearing and respect. Few things offend him more than the sight of a man wearing a T-shirt to a wedding or a funeral.

I love visiting my dad—it's like a trip back in time. The

kitchen is the masterpiece, my favorite room in the house, an architectural paean to the brash optimism of my childhood years, the period when our family was at its most raucous, its most brilliantly implosive, yet somehow still intact. The appliances are mustard gold, without a single digital touchpad except on the microwave, which is the one cooking device that sees a fair bit of action. And the wine fridge, which is kept at a precise temperature and houses my dad's collection of vintage bottles. A stove with chrome knobs and coil elements. A gurgling refrigerator with double doors and a nonfunctioning ice machine. It all still works, or kind of works, an astounding testament to the longevity of goods constructed before our throwaway times.

This room has never been remodeled because my father has never cooked, despite knowing the exact preparation methods of a global array of dishes, many of which he has sampled during his extensive travels. I've never seen my father operate a can opener or even boil water. I tell myself he must perform these operations behind my back, but when I'm in his kitchen, it's the one place he won't enter, not even to pass through, as if our mutual presence in this room breaks some kind of covenant. He was born in a traditional Indian household, raised to eat food cooked by others, to be shooed from the slicing and dicing.

The kitchen is at the back of the house and has just one little window, a setback rectified by a sunshine ceiling, an uninterrupted bank of fluorescent lights covered with pebbled plastic panels. When I flick the switch, the room illuminates with an unrepentant blast of cheery light. I appreciate this devotion to the bright side, despite the odds, which is my dad's position also.

The kitchen drawers are full of mystery keys, golf balls,

charging cables, manuals for defunct technology, and cigar cutters. For a long time he assured me he didn't smoke, or had given it up, yet despite these promises I find the accoutrements of his hobby everywhere. But I never find any actual cigars.

Just as I'm finishing up with the broom, I hear the garage door ratchet up on its tracks. I listen for the thunk of the car door. After a time, he pushes the kitchen door open and announces first thing that he is sore. His therapist pushed him a little too hard today. My dad used to walk around with his hands in his pockets, jingling the loose change, but now he moves with his hands out to the railings, the wainscotting, the furniture in order to steady himself.

"Charlotte," he says, pronouncing my name without the central R. "Don't ever get old." He still has a foreigner's accent, but because I'm his daughter, I don't really hear it. I understand every word he says.

"Cup of tea?" I ask.

"That would be nice," he replies before disappearing into the living room.

I stop what I'm doing at once. I fill the kettle and locate his favorite cookies in the cupboard. It's a style of doting I don't do for anyone else on the planet, not even my own husband. My dad lives alone. I'm his chauffeur, housekeeper, and dining companion when I'm visiting, which is something I do quite a bit, despite the fact that for twenty years we didn't talk at all.

COLONIAL  LOVE

MY MOTHER IS WHITE. SHE'S ENGLISH, OR AT least England was where she was born and raised. Like my father, she'll never go back to where she came from—even if she's never received this as a directive. She's North American now. She's also Catholic. She has gray eyes, silver hair, and is one of the most fair-skinned people I know. My mother lives in Ontario near the broad, flat banks of the St. Lawrence River in a brick bungalow with her second husband, a normal guy who couldn't be more different from my father. Their village is a place that couldn't be more different from her ancestral home; the only things these two places share are a lapping shore and the late queen's face on all the money.

My mother's origin story is like a movie about the fading gentry, about people who go sailing and swimming in the frigid North Atlantic, who get about in mended tweed and

Wellington boots and cook for themselves on their servants' day off. My grandfather's name was Reginald, and that was the gist of his childhood. He grew up in an old mansion with two staircases, one for the family and one for the help, and little bells in the kitchen, like those in the scullery in *Downton Abbey*. But my great-grandfather died when Reg was just a boy, and after that, the golden years and the family fortune began to drain away. This has been a lasting motif, the voyage from riches to rags.

My grandmother came from nothing, from grinding poverty, in the days before national assistance, socialized healthcare, or council housing in the UK. She was born in a workhouse, institutions that housed the elderly, the infirm, and the poor—meager, loveless places for children, if *Oliver Twist* is to be believed. Her father, a ghostly presence whom I suppose I should call my great-grandfather, died when she was very young. When her mother remarried, little Phyllis was cast off, sent to live at a convent, for all intents orphaned by her own penniless kin. She was raised by nuns, converting to Catholicism in the process. My grandmother never told anyone the full details of this upbringing, not even her own husband, a secret shame she carried to her grave. The truth was discovered later by my mother and her sister, who came across a birth certificate while conducting a genealogical hunt. Their mother's real name wasn't Phyllis; it was Ethel. She had been renamed at some point during her childhood, and she'd used this pseudonym her whole life to avoid the classist stigma, real or perceived, of her origins. She'd passed herself off as a completely different person than the one listed in her documents and written in her DNA, like an impostor in her own life.

My mother was born into a soup of poverty consciousness in the middle of World War II. But right from the beginning she was ambitious and smart, as if in defiance of her humble beginnings. She hated her mother as a begrudged ice queen who favored her younger daughter, my aunt, whose fair-haired prettiness mirrored Grandma Phyllis's looks. My mother aligned instead with her father, who was bookish, introverted, and residually worldly, despite the fact that for most of his married life, he never traveled much at all. My grandmother had been a party girl who'd worked as a hotel receptionist, but once married, she settled down to a life of child-rearing, washing up, and chain-smoking in between. Traditional femininity held no appeal for my mother, at least not as a defining identity, no promise at all for her future. As a teenager she left home for London and entered the medical school track. She was always going to be a doctor. She never wanted to do anything else.

When my mother was a child, everyone was listening to Vera Lynn on the wireless, but by the time she came of age it was the Beatles, Mary Quant, and Apollo missions to the moon. The baby boomers became teenagers, a generation hell-bent on exuberant revolution. The spirit is captured in Michelangelo Antonioni's *Blow-Up,* the iconic sixties movie that follows its photographer protagonist through London's revolving-door worlds, its high-gloss fashion scene and countercultural hedonism contrasted with the gritty realities of life in its more downtrodden neighborhoods. My parents met in this moment, a time straddling two ways of seeing and being, one eager to devour the future, the other glancing back. One rocketing up to the stratosphere, one struggling up from the ditch.

· · ·

BY THE TIME my dad showed up in London, immigrants from Commonwealth nations had been arriving steadily for decades, craving the same prosperity and opportunity the English had sought to reap from their far colonial shores. At home, they'd absorbed the messages of British propaganda such as *Springtime in an English Village,* a film shown throughout African and Caribbean colonies in a campaign to draw cheap labor. The movie depicted roomy pastoral landscapes and utopic schools in which brown children learn harmoniously alongside white kids, and a Black girl is taught to curtsy before she's crowned May queen.

Upon arrival they were quickly disabused of the illusion. England was not the prosperous, mighty nation their colonial masters had built up in imagination. Instead, they discovered a small, drizzly island struggling to rebuild after two wars. Nor were they showered with rose petals by their new English neighbors. Immigrants of color faced housing discrimination and were often forced into cramped, expensive, rat-infested accommodations, if they could get white landlords to rent to them at all. They were ineligible for government subsidies, since five years of residency were required before one could apply for a council flat.

Many immigrants had spent their lives as Anglophones and subjects of the queen, steeped in British culture, believing themselves to be citizens with all the same rights and privileges as natural-born Britons. But not even fifteen years after the doors had been opened, the influx was met with public alarm, and Parliament began to pass laws, each more restrictive than the last, to nudge them shut. Before long you needed a prearranged job before you could arrive, not just a suitcase and a pocket full of hope. Still, thousands came in the postwar years before 1971, when the Immigration Act would strictly limit who could reside in the United Kingdom, even—and especially—colonials with British passports. Migrants from Caribbean countries were especially hard-hit. Untallied thousands were granted residency, but the Home Office tracked no names and issued no official documents, exposing these new arrivals to deportation, economic hardship, and homelessness for decades after. An entire generation got trapped in the legal cracks in English citizenship, a disenfranchisement that remains unresolved to this day.

Sikhs were part of this postwar wave, and they endured their own share of cultural opposition. Many Sikh men had fought for England during the war, their turbans an accepted part of their military uniforms, but in this new ecosystem they faced workplace bans that required them to shave their beards and cut their hair, in effect forcing them to choose between the sacred articles of the faith and the laws of their new land.

But the Empire was always a multiheaded creature, a phenomenon of both affinity and repulsion. Welcome for the foreign-born seemed to expand and shrink like sea ice, depending on the economic needs of the mother country, or the flavor of the government of the day, or public sentiment toward all those extra brown bodies. My father received a medical scholarship when the country was aggressively recruiting foreign healthcare workers, a move to address personnel shortages in the newly formed National Health Service. But unlike his working-class contemporaries elsewhere in the UK, my dad got away with wearing a turban, at least for a little while. In London, he moved into "digs," as he calls them still, chilly, rented rooms with coin-operated fireplaces ruled by grumbling, quietly racist landladies. As far as I can tell, this was one of two periods in his life when he had little to no money.

My father was unused to scrimping by. He was born in India but grew up in Nairobi when Kenya was still a British territory. My grandfather was a successful businessman under foreign rule, what you might call Raj-adjacent. He made a thriving enterprise of furniture manufacturing and lived comfortably with my grandmother and their expansive brood in a big house with an avocado tree in the yard. My dad attended the Duke of Gloucester, a high school that's still operational today, albeit under a significantly less colonial name, a whitewashed building with arches and columns, and palm trees in the center of the circular drive. My grandparents spoke Punjabi, but at the Duke of Gloucester my dad was taught in English by instructors of British extraction, "Anglos," which is still his word for white people. Kenya's South Asian population was technically African, but they lived in a highly stratified, segregated society. They seldom mixed with the Kikuyu, Maasai, or any of the indigenous peoples whose ancestral lands they'd settled alongside the British, a cultural and political alignment that would contribute to their exodus later on.

In 1963, Kenya declared its independence from Queen Elizabeth II and, in the ensuing years, began implementing Africanization policies. The streets were renamed and the systems undone that kept Africans sidelined and restricted, including the abolition of the Empire's most oppressive symbol, the kipande, an identification locket box worn around the neck by a chain, which had been mandatory for African men. A couple hundred thousand Kenyan Asians had built lives in the former East Africa Protectorate, and many had been born there, but they knew their days of favor were numbered. Foreseeing an Indian influx, British Parliament rushed in a new immigration bill further tightening rights of abode for subjects of the Crown. Now one needed to be born on English soil or have at least one parent or grandparent who could claim that privilege, in effect closing the border to most Commonwealth citizens of non-Anglo descent. But my dad, thanks to his serendipitously well-timed medical training, had already sailed his way between the wandering rocks. And just like that, he pulled off what he has somehow always managed to do—pass unscathed through the tiny rips in history.

I SOMETIMES WONDER about the kismet that brought them together, why the daughter of an English bank manager found a bearded, turban-wearing foreigner with a thick Indo-Kenyan accent so appealing, and vice versa. Maybe attraction is an involuntary impulse, even if it's the opposite of what our parents say we should want, which often enough is to stick to our own kind. My mother thought my dad was the most handsome man she'd ever met. Today my dad seldom mentions matters of the heart with Western abandon, but beyond his reticence, it's as if their memories of romance have been all but obliterated, dissolved by the strife that followed them through their marriage.

Maybe it was the sixties that brought them together—in many ways, a rebellious time. By my parents' reports, London was a groovy place back then. But a stubborn conservatism lurked beneath all the progress. The culture was barely prepared for its first waves of reverse colonization let alone to claim chicken tikka masala as the national dish. It was definitely not ready to accept a white woman married to a very brown man from a country whose independence had been "granted" just a dozen years before.

But my mother never worried about what people thought. She became an anesthesiologist when it was conceptually freaky, even transgressive, for a woman to do so. She married my father when interracial relationships were uncommon. But I think she got a crash course in intolerance in those early days. When she walked with my dad in the streets, she'd get elbowed in the chest and shoved off the sidewalk. She learned there's a special variety of prejudice reserved for an Indian cocky enough to marry an Englishwoman. And for a white woman who steps out of line.

In the decades leading up to my parents' marriage, a brown face in a white crowd wasn't likely to raise many eyebrows. Nor was it bound to please everyone. But often enough, it inspired the attentions of local women, who received the UK's new arrivals—many of them migrant workers from the colonies who were also male and single—without any of the common prejudices of the day. The ensuing romances triggered alarm in the white establishment and the media, who dipped into troves of racist sensationalism to explain this shocking cross-pollination. According to those depictions, Indians were morally and physically weak, equally as liable to commit bribery as to tell lies in order to achieve their ends. They were also lascivious perverts, themselves the products of unnatural couplings, the sons of polygamous fathers and child brides.

Despite all the smelling salts, Britons were well acquainted with interracial romance, if not on their own soil, then depicted in popular culture. Many plays, films, and pulp novels of the early twentieth century featured dalliances between white protagonists and sexually available brown colonials with the Empire for a backdrop, sexy-ugly liaisons that usually ended in tragedy, rejection, or some kind of punishment for the foreign supporting actor. If you were a male member of the British aristocracy married to a Chinese heiress, or an actress betrothed to an Indian prince, you might receive favorable public attention as an upper-class exoticism. But this latitude didn't necessarily extend to the people of the neighborhood. At street level, the reaction to mixed love was practically emetic. As Sir Ralph Williams, a former colonial governor, wrote in 1919: "It is an instinctive certainty that sexual relations between white women and colored men revolt our very nature." Interracial love was not only corrosive to civilized society, but also powerfully nauseating, something close to monstrous in its imagined intimacies.

Moral anxiety around interracial unions didn't apply to white men, powerful ones especially, whose unquestioned dominance had been the norm. For them, social firewalls between ruler and subordinate meant little when it came to sexual entitlement, especially out in far-flung colonies. For the working classes back home, the influx of foreign workers inflamed a resource-guarding aggression; the "stealing" of women by "colored" foreigners became a proxy for the theft of jobs and housing from rightful heirs. When a white woman and a Black man stepped out in public together, it often brought the threat of physical violence, and for quite a while, it could also incite a rumble.

Collective fretting over international love eventually found its way into laws deterring those unions, with pinpoint focus on couplings between men of color and white women. An Englishwoman gutsy or foolish enough to marry a foreign-born "alien" was forced to surrender her nationality by order of the British Nationality and Status of Aliens Act—a law that didn't apply to men and remained in place until 1948.

But as my parents' orbits collided, life was changing fast. In the decades after the war, it was as if the map of the world had been ripped up and redrawn, its old pieces shaken and tossed up into the air to fall wherever they might. The days of ethnic homogeneity in Europe seemed to be over. The colonies were dissolving along with Britain's sense of its own national power, an existential earthquake for many who'd spent their whole lives believing the sun never set on the Empire. This was the zeitgeist, the world my parents inherited. The colonials had come home to roost.

FOR MY DAD, an alliance with my mother represented acceptance and entrée, despite its risks, a way of blending into his adopted world. But he must have symbolized the opposite to my mother—an exit from the stifling confines of conventional life, which never appealed to her in the first place. They were both climbers, progressive beyond the fishbowl constraints of their natal worlds. He married an English physician who'd wear a lab coat a thousand times before she ever put on a salwar kameez. She married a brown man in the face of the sexist, classist traditions that she despised. But no matter how easy or difficult their courtship had been, they faced similar headwinds at work.

He loved the United Kingdom. But he also hated what he considered the British talent for obsequious smackdowns. When he worked in England, his hospital colleagues would kill him with kindness and then laugh behind his back, or maybe stab him there if he got too ambitious. Or they'd flip the joke right out in the open, expecting he'd take it lying down. But he had little talent for diplomatic compliance. Appendectomies were his skill, along with pacemakers, bowel resections, and hernia repair. "Those bloody bastards," he says, even now.

Discrimination was just an expected denominator for my dad and his brown colleagues, who faced promotional obstacles and hierarchies with mysterious inner workings. Foreigners were easy enough to identify and eliminate in a stack of applications—the Singhs, the Khans, the Patels. Immigrant doctors could send out sheaves of résumés while their white contemporaries were hired after just a few tries. They got stuck in junior loops, working in specialties they didn't want, often for considerably less pay. They were consigned to rural areas, or districts where British-born doctors didn't care to go. You could be a Nobel Prize laureate, it seemed, and yet still find yourself working twenty lifetimes as a geriatrician in the rocky outlands of the British Isles, far beyond the embrace of your community. No matter where you found yourself in the hospital, there was always something in the way, some force pulling you down by the pant leg. It was hard to talk about, this invisible energy, even if you saw it from the corner of your eye. It was just like a fog—pervasive but untouchable, evaporating before you could even give it a name.

Meanwhile, my mother faced occupational hazards of her own. She posed for her medical school class photos amid rows and rows of men, the odd woman nearly disappearing in the masculine tableaux. Back then there was no maternity leave. When my mother announced she was pregnant with twins, her colleagues tried to make her quit by stationing her in the X-ray room with nothing but a lead apron for protection. So she left, just as they wanted, but set her sights on a better job—and a better life—that she knew must exist out there somewhere.

WHEN MY MOTHER announced she was marrying a Sikh man, the shock of it just about made her parents' hair fall out. But my grandfather had spent years in the Merchant Navy, much of it with Indian crew, albeit as their superior. If he disapproved of the union, it didn't last forever. He wasn't about to sacrifice his relationship with his daughter by clinging to the idea of the proper English bloke she should have married. But I'll bet my grandmother had a hell of a time with it. I remember her as an unaffectionate woman with a helmet of butterscotch curls and the comportment of a duchess gone down to the gutter. Not a whiff of grand-motherly love exists in my memory of her.

My father chose a white bride, which is key to the shape of his life, my mother's, and our entire branch of the family tree. He was the firstborn son. Traditionally, a prodigal Indian man returns to his father's house on the understanding he will marry and continue to live with his parents, plowing whatever investment has been made in his upbringing and education back into the household. To escape, to follow one's individualized dreams is perfectly reasonable in the West, even recommended. But in Indian culture it's a bit like embezzling your parents' retirement savings to buy a red Mercedes convertible, which by the way is the car my father still drives, pretty unstoppably, even now.

My father and his father didn't speak for decades, not until my grandfather was very frail and, as it turned out, on his deathbed. In the intervening years, I never met either of my grandparents. The day my parents met, that's when our family cracked. It's the point where my mother, father, and their three children broke off from the past and began our drift across the ocean.

HALF-CASTES IN 3 WONDERLAND

SHE LIKED ORDER, PUNCTUALITY, AND INDEX CARDS neatly hand-printed with lists. He eschewed schedules and left piles of clothing dotted around on their bedroom floor.

She liked to swim. The only place he got wet was the shower.

She woke up at dawn—and often long before sunrise in the middle of winter. He preferred to stay up late, then sleep in whenever he could get away with it.

She didn't mind a tuna sandwich. He preferred veal scaloppine.

My parents approached their shared life like envoys from two distant planets, but at least they had doctoring in common. And then they had us, their mid-toned offspring, acquired two for the price of one, which presented a new kind of difference.

During her pregnancy, my mother received plenty of unsolicited advice. *Think of the children,* people said. Mixed-race offspring would suffer nothing but disadvantage due to the reckless nuptial choices of their parents. Then my twin and I were born in London in the middle of winter, seventeen minutes apart. Of course, there was nothing wrong with us. We were healthy, rotund infants with dark hair and brown eyes. But we looked nothing like our mother. She'd get stopped on the street by strangers as she pushed us around in a stroller. "How good of you," they'd say, "to adopt those little brown babies."

Not long after that, as if our gestation was the only remaining hitch, my parents left the United Kingdom for good. We made the transatlantic flight as babes in straw baskets, Moses-style, as per our mother's tastes, which for many years trended toward the natural-fibered and the whole-grained—toward roughage in general, you could say.

My parents knew the fog and the gloaming of the British Isles, but not the relentless assaults of winter in the Atlantic provinces of Canada—a witch's brew of damp, blustery maritime influences stirred in with arctic lows. During the first chilly autumn in Nova Scotia, our mother inquired of her new hospital colleagues: *Does it get any colder than this?* They doubled over in laughter, but she had no idea why. At first, Canada was an alien biosphere characterized by infant snowsuits, car engine block heaters, and forced-air furnaces. During storms, pedestrians on street corners clung to one another while waiting for the lights to change, for fear of being blown out into traffic. A few months later, the ocean froze over. Our parents had never seen anything like it.

She went out and bought herself a red wool Hudson's

Bay parka with a fur-trimmed hood. He refused the humiliations of proper Canadian outerwear, opting instead for a double-breasted sheepskin coat in a style Dr. Zhivago might have worn, even if it outweighed him whenever it got wet. But almost from the very beginning my twin and I were North American kids. As we grew, we'd tunnel in snowbanks, never questioning our frozen eyelashes and nostril hairs. Cold became our element, our native substrate. In the summer, we'd learn to stay in swimming pools until our lips turned blue.

My father was still wearing a turban, although right around then he untied it. Traditionally, Sikhs don't cut their hair as a sign of respect for the way God made them. But the weight of those six yards of fabric was heavy, and he knew it well by then. This was often the price of entry to the promised land—your lifetime, measured out in inches of hair. For many years, my mother kept my father's shorn locks wrapped in a paper towel at the back of her jewelry drawer, right next to his old, defunct passport.

My dad knew that the rigidly faithful and the unassimilated pay an extra toll for taking up space in the West. That's why my first name, which he chose expressly, isn't Harpreet or Jatinder but that of a dead British queen. My brother is named with similar majesty after Alexander the Great, the Macedonian king who once invaded Punjab, but no matter. This is the sort of grand destiny our father had in mind for us—a source of self-satire, as it would turn out, more than any kind of inspiration.

My dad spent his childhood on the big Nairobi estate with the avocado tree in the yard. My mother knew the rooms and hallways of a crumbling ancestral mansion. She could probably still find her way in a blindfold from its lawns to the shores of the Atlantic Ocean. But after the move to Canada, houses would cease to mean anything deep or nostalgic. There would be no kitchen doorjamb that kept all our height markings. No handprints pushed into wet cement. No backyard shrines to deceased family pets.

For the first few years of Canadian life, our family bounced around the Atlantic provinces. St. John's, Moncton, Halifax. We lived in a series of dwellings, mostly rented. These were like hermit crab shells, merely places to occupy, the vacated spaces of other families. These houses are lost to my memory, confined to the hundreds of photos my mother keeps, album-bound, in a storage room at the back of her basement. My parents tried to get a grip on this new world, to navigate the bureaucracies of immigration, including repeating their board exams. It wasn't always easy to find two jobs in the same city that suited their training. On the other hand, they were utterly free from any kind of family meddling. But it must have felt like floating in space, their only lifeline to each other, with us in the middle.

OUR MOTHER SPENT her professional life in the witness of birth and death, but despite this, or maybe because of it, she was soft as a jellyfish when it came to parenting. She had no stomach at all for discipline. My brother and I were like two infant orangutans, and many childhood photos feature us in perpetual motion, our limbs caught in a blur. We crawled over the floor, the furniture, over her shoulders, competing for access to her lap, which she encouraged with fake exasperation. Our father was more interested in strictures, but he was also changeable, fickle with his attentions. Our chaos was enough to test his patience, but it had less to do with our future comportment and more with his present tense. Even then we knew he had nothing on us. Our mother was a goner for her kids.

Surely my dad never questioned the idea of himself as a husband and father, just as my mother always thought she'd become a wife and mother. It was simply expected—a duty to kin, tradition, society. But I doubt for a millisecond he foresaw himself as a modern, participatory dad with babies in two arms and burp cloths on either shoulder. No one could leave a room like he could at the first sign of a whimper or a meltdown. Hands-on fatherhood was a strange Western quirk to him. He'd received his family-relations cues not from feminism or even practical household reality, but from my grandparents, who, despite living abroad, had imported the generational ways of the Punjabi village, their culture frozen in Edwardian amber.

If it was exhausting to be a medical resident with grinding shifts and rotations, the sleep hours only got shorter when my mother became a full-time working mom with emergency surgeries in the middle of the night. She had two babies and no one to lean on, not a single cousin or distant aunt nearby. This is how I think of our mother during our childhood—sleep deprived, seldom alone, with too much to do and never enough hours in the day. Possibly she'd done all this math in advance. Maybe my parents had already discussed their separate expectations and wildly divergent traditions yet still decided to make the leap. After all, who really knows what they're going to get when they sign up for the adventure of family life?

Whatever dreams existed, they must have paled at three in the morning with babies fussing in the room next door. How many clarifying moments owed themselves not to character flaws or personal failings but to the slow, tectonic collision of worlds and cultures, or the true, belated costs of leaving home? Our parents were conducting an experiment in international relations with few precedents and no guidebook. They left everything they'd known in the rearview mirror, and everything their parents had known as well.

BACK IN THE DAY, if a woman was stymied by the vicissitudes of mothering, she asked a friend, or maybe her own mother for help. But Grandma Phyllis lived an ocean away, possibly by design, and long-distance phone minutes cost as much as a rover mission to Mars. But even if Phyllis had lived right next door, I doubt my mother would have consulted her about a single domestic matter—beyond the making of ice cubes with a cryogenic touch of a finger. Our mother had none of that frosty temperament. She was a warm and abundant caregiver despite receiving little physical affection herself in childhood. No matter what transpired at work, we were the best part of her day, or at least she made us feel like we were.

For advice, there was always the child-rearing bible of her generation, *The Common Sense Book of Baby and Child Care* by Dr. Benjamin Spock. The message reinforced our mother's intuitive parenting, including her forward-thinking belief that babies should not be left to cry themselves to sleep, or really be left to cry at all during early infancy, when every squeak or whimper might be explained by a predictable array of culprits, such as hunger or a wet diaper. According to Dr. Spock, babies should be breastfed on demand, which presented her with the herculean task of feeding two mouths while employed full-time. She'd returned to work

only weeks after we were born, leaving us in the daytime
with a series of nannies—a reality that seems distantly
strange to me now. Dr. Spock did not approve of babysitters
or outsourced childcare. "It doesn't make sense," he wrote
at the time, "to let mothers go to work making dresses in a
factory or tapping typewriters in an office, and have them
pay other people to do a poorer job of bringing up their
children."

Spock's title was a massive bestseller that launched the
parenting-book industry. But if you needed assistance in the
raising of half-brown kids back in the day, you were out of
luck in the bookstore. By the time the first self-help guides
on the subject of multiethnic child-rearing appeared, my
brother and I had already graduated from high school. It
was too late for any kind of sage or celebrative advice. The
water had flowed—it had flooded—beneath the bridge.

If there were no parenting titles, it wasn't because mixed-
race children didn't exist, it was because books on the subject had been stored not in Child Psychology, but in other,
more primatological sections of the library. In the decades—
indeed the centuries—before I was born, people thought of
hybrid offspring not as a natural part of human evolution,
but as biologically exotic aberrations.

Before the twentieth century, if you were of mixed race,
you were a degenerate—weak, disease-prone, destined for a
short, tragic life. Half-caste offspring, as they were often
known, were described in zoological terms as "piebald" or
"mongrel." "Mulattoes" were believed to produce no offspring, just as mules, crossbred from donkeys and horses,
were infertile. Because they were reproductively unviable,
they would simply die out, or be killed by their own clans.
So went the prevailing wisdom, despite evidence to the con-

trary in seemingly every corner of the colonized globe, including the plantation, where white men regularly fathered children with enslaved women as a matter of personal and economic right. The logical contortion and workaround explanation in such cases was that white sperm was superior, with a potency capable of negating the deleterious effects of interbreeding.

Despite their inborn deficiencies, half-bloods still had the power to pollute the intelligent design of God, for whom perfection could only mean whiteness. Ideas like these showed up in the work of nineteenth-century French ethnologist Arthur de Gobineau, whose influential philosophy of racial determinism held that whites were beautiful, strong, and intelligent, while other races were savage, stupid, and ugly. Mixing would lead not only to the dilution of princely white blood, but ultimately to societal upheaval: "When the mediocre men are once created at the expense of the greater, they combine with other mediocrities, and from such unions, which grow ever more and more degraded, is born a confusion which, like that of Babel, ends in utter impotence, and leads societies down to the abyss of nothingness whence no power on earth can rescue them."

De Gobineau was no lone wolf; he was the recipient of a long and plentiful tradition. From the moment European conquerors planted flags on foreign shores, oceans of ink were spilled by white intellectual luminaries on the subject of racial difference. They catalogued the great kaleidoscope of humanity by flesh tone. Red, white, yellow, and black. Americanus, Europeanus, Asiaticus, and Africanus. White, Negro, Hun, Hindu. Yellow, Copper, Tawny, Black. These taxonomies varied depending on the epoch, but invariably, whiteness appeared at the top. Caucasians were not only

physically unique but also different in native temperament—
more civilized, more attractive, smarter—the descendants of
Adam and Eve. People of color formed separate breeds, an
idea underwritten by polygenism, the belief that the Black
race in particular was a distinct species, descended from a
parallel evolutionary lineage.

Polygenism found its heyday in the nineteenth century,
coinciding with the rise of "racial science," the purportedly
empirical study of racial classification through the measure-
ment of human body parts. Scientists and doctors of the En-
lightenment poked and prodded brown bodies, performing
dissections in the cases of the deceased, in search of definitive physiological differences between white and dark skin.
They collected vast troves of human skulls, measuring foreheads, eye sockets, and nasal cavities in the hopes of proving
the design discrepancies between races. The goal was to
build a race pyramid, or rather to buttress a Caucasian
upper tier, even if investigators never met any of the people
they consigned to the bottom strata. The details may have
been hotly debated, but the fundamentals remained unquestioned until Darwin's work on evolution came to prominence.

By the twentieth century, the allures of scientific racism
were fading, but the anxiety over half-caste children per-
sisted. During my grandparents' generation, few may have
said outright that mixed children were a bestial abomina-
tion, but still their plight fell under the purview of social
work and philanthropy. To forestall their further suffering,
it was believed that multiracial children should be sterilized
at birth, a philosophy expounded by the Society for Con-
structive Birth Control and Racial Progress, a group formed

in the UK in 1921. The Society's founders were early promoters of birth control, a progressive feminist idea had it not been tied to eugenics. These ideas began to die off—officially anyway—in the postwar period after the horrors of the Nazi project had been revealed. But old notions like these have remarkable survivability, even when they've become obsolete, even when they were never true to begin with.

Perhaps no one in the twentieth century made better trade in the academic investigation of mixedness than Everett Stonequist, an American sociologist whose 1937 book, *The Marginal Man,* was devoted to the subject of hybrid blood through the observation of global groups, among them the Cape Colored of South Africa, "mulattoes" of the United States, and the Eurasians of India, who featured as outcasts, rejected by both Indians and the English alike. According to Stonequist, "mixed bloods" inherited the weakest traits of their parents, and as a consequence were destined for mediocrity. They had a natural tendency toward racial anxiety, not to mention keen status consciousness and persecution complexes. They were prone to shapeshifting, aligning with whiteness whenever it was convenient. According to Stonequist, "The mixed blood's first impulse is to identify himself with the race which is considered superior."

Stonequist's ideas emphasized mediocrity and maladjustment. Pinned between worlds, a product of two parental ethnicities but accepted by neither, the half-caste's woes were everybody's trouble. "Because of these peculiarities the mixed blood presents a special problem for the community: what is to be his place in the social organization? As he matures he too will become aware of his problematic and anomalous social position. He will become the target of whatever hostile sentiments exist between the parent races. Thus his problem of adjustment will be made more acute."

Stonequist didn't concern himself much at all with non-Caucasian combinations. As with so many scholars, it was the white factor that drew his fascination. Stonequist's half-bloods were just as confused as de Gobineau's. Their problem was not a racialized world, nor its resulting factions, but rather the personal mysteries of a pathological birthright. Even today, the idea of mixedness as a form of zebroid humanity, somehow confused by its own stripes, traces back to Stonequist and other scholars like him.

Stonequist took it for granted that Caucasians were "considered superior" but stopped just shy of saying they actually were—biologically, genetically, and even spiritually supreme. But in many ways, he didn't need to say it. Those ideas had been lurking around for eons, had been stated as fact for hundreds of years before they eventually, reluctantly, slid from polite discourse, if not totally out of the ether.

4 LIMBO

SHE WAS A CONFIRMED CATHOLIC, A DIRECT RESULT of the nuns who had raised my granny in the poorhouse. He was Sikh, about as far as one could get from priestly vestments and swinging censers. But according to both religions, marriage was sacrosanct. Family was the fabric of society, marriage and parenthood the knitting that held everything together.

She believed in God and the heavens.

My father had no template for an anthropomorphized all-father with smiting powers and underworld adversaries. He'd grown up with an abstract godhead that was one and the same with creation, that enveloped humanity and the world completely and so could never be truly known. Sikhism taught five virtues: truth, compassion, contentment, humility, and love. These were mirrored quite simply by the five thieves: lust, wrath, greed, attachment, and pride.

Catholicism perplexed my father. On the one hand, you had the seven deadly sins, which were not to be confused with mortal sins such as murder—those were separate. But earthly crimes, no matter how grave, could be absolved by simply stepping into the phone booth of the confessional and coming clean. My mother believed in turning the other cheek, according to the teachings of Jesus. My dad believed in sacrifice—to a point. If you were pushed too far, it became acceptable, even mandatory, to fight back. It was right there in the branding, the Sikh symbol of the khanda, which features three swords crossed with a sharpened throwing ring.

If my mother had had her way, my middle name would be Mary, and she'd keep photos of me dressed as a little bride of Jesus in a white communion dress. I would have attended private schools with the words "Assumption" or "Sacred Heart" in their names. I'd have spent the better part of my childhood in a blazer, tie, and kilt. But my dad didn't want his children going anywhere near the church—this was expressly verboten—or being schooled in the ways of "the Man God," as he calls the Lord Jesus to this day.

Nevertheless, our mother had her subterfuge. If you can't go straight through, go around or go under—a skill we learned from her. Whenever we asked how she spent her days, the occupation that kept her away during our waking hours, she said she *put people to sleep*. I didn't understand that she was a healthcare professional trained in the implementation of narcotic substances. Instead, I believed she was some kind of tuck-in expert, a blanket turner or pillow fluffer for other kids or even, I supposed, sick adults in need of nurturing attention. Bedtime was our favorite daily phase, since we had our mother all to ourselves; it seemed reasonable that others would appreciate this, too.

She'd still be dressed for work in her wool skirts and cowl-neck sweaters, perhaps freshly arrived through the front door, yet she'd come upstairs before she'd gotten a chance to eat her own dinner. She bathed us every night, even though, with two human otters in the tub, this was an unavoidably humid affair for the lifeguard. She supervised our toothbrushing and hair detangling and, after that, climbed into bed with us to read Bible stories on the sly. This part of the evening remained totally immune to fatherly scrutiny, since he was on the couch downstairs, watching the news of the world, much as he does today. This was something she did only when our dad wasn't around, an unspoken secret among the three of us.

She read to us from children's stories and occasionally from the *Good News Bible,* whose psychedelic sunset cover and onion-skin paper were a fixture on her bedside table for years. We began in the obvious place, with the life of baby Jesus, who was cool by us because of his adjacency to Christmas and Santa. Christmas was our favorite commercial blowout of the year, even though we'd been forbidden from attending midnight mass and half of our parental unit had spent his own youth celebrating Diwali. The Mediterranean landscapes of Judea were the opposite of our Canadian setting, but the story's themes of family vagrancy felt familiar, at least in broad strokes. Mary was engaged to Joseph, but before they could seal the deal, she experienced a visitation from the angel Gabriel, who announced to her: *You are about to become heavy with child.*

The subject of reproduction held the same appeal as the

plain Corn Flakes in a variety pack of Kellogg's cereal. We had medical parents, and the origination of babies was described to us in a terribly dull blizzard of cellular, anatomically correct detail. Still, the nativity story presented several troubling riddles. Who was this impregnating Lord but a terrifying force, according to our mother, who knew the precise number of hairs on our heads and saw everything we did, like a hovering surveillance satellite? He was endowed with huge, beguiling power, yet mostly did not stoop to the level of regular earthlings.

It was only natural to make a connection between the heavenly father and the one in our own house, even if this was an imprecise corollary. Our dad was a shadowy force in our lives. Like a ship's captain, he directed our overarching family trajectory, yet his specific parental function was the subject of speculation. He didn't figure into the minutiae of feeding or bathing, nor was he concerned with our nutrient intake or when we were meant to visit the dentist. When it came to the facts of his children's lives, he swung widely between total oblivion and searing scrutiny with few intermediate stops in between. He seemed surprised each time we crawled or crashed into his presence, as if shocked that a small set of humans could produce such a big blast radius of disorder and mayhem. When he entered a room, the molecules shifted, changed directions in the air. He could be testy, a thundering presence who lacked our mother's love for our comedy as well as her inexhaustible patience. But his proximity did not run on any kind of timetable; he had a schedule that was all his own.

In other bedtime stories, we learned of mortal trials. To test Abraham's obedience, God commanded Abraham to sacrifice his only child, Isaac. Abraham tied his boy to the altar and prepared for the ritual to be carried out by his own hand. The point of the ordeal was a test of Abraham's faith, and Isaac was spared at the last moment. But in this story, we identified vehemently not with the father but with the boy. In this nightmare scenario, it seemed reasonable to assume that Isaac would be scared witless by the vision of his trusted and beloved dad sharpening the blade intended for his neck. Wouldn't he always be horribly triggered, forever after, when his dad ventured near a rope or a knife?

Next came the story of Cain and Abel with its troubling themes of sibling rivalry and violent fratricide—more than slightly unsettling given the proximal nature of our own twinship. Ours was an unspoken language; we could read the other's emotions with a glance. But squabbles came as naturally to us as brushing our teeth together in front of the bathroom mirror. Our genetic codes were not identical, but we'd shared the same womb and now were trapped in developmental lockstep. We shared the same bedroom. We split gifts and birthday cakes. We were known as "the twins." We experienced nearly every second of life as a single unit. We didn't always play together; we played side by side, or more often, back-to-back, a form of privacy where none existed elsewhere. Old Testament or not, the underlying message of Cain and Abel seemed to touch on the short line between love and revenge, closeness and recrimination.

Immortality was for divinities only, but what happened to normal people when they died? They went to heaven, our mother explained, which seemed like an abundant place with sunshine, puppies, and free-flowing Coke where no one got in trouble for backtalking or refusing to eat their vegetables. You had to be good to go to heaven, which seemed like a slippery, elite designation. If you were bad you went to hell, described to us by our mother in evasive terms as a place where cravings were never sated and itches could never be scratched.

We learned about the afterlife from TV, a verboten device as decreed by our father, even though he watched it himself. As did we. We sat before the screen at point-blank range, soaking up its blue rays with copious abandon whenever he was out of the house. Hell was depicted in our favorite cartoons, a place with trapdoors that opened to underground caverns of soot and torment. Here guilty dogs and cats were boiled alive in cauldrons, or lowered into blazing conflagrations, each flame alive, animated, and diabolically sentient. It was just like the tree of knowledge in the Garden of Eden—true learning, it seemed, was always tied to a hidden crime.

Christmas was followed by mysterious, unnamed rituals, secretly honored by our mother. She quietly returned to the house with dabs of ash on her forehead or wizened palm fronds given as favors from some kind of grave event she had attended without us, all on her own.

By then our mother had been forced to reveal a disturbing tenet. To get into heaven, you also had to be baptized, a rite involving blessings and the dribbling of holy water over a baby's forehead. This water was extra special, according to my interpretation—heavy, steeped in magic. Our mother had been the recipient of this mystical rite, but we had not been, according to our father's wishes. What would happen to us, then?

We found out there was yet another realm for cases such as ours. We were destined for a floating space in between heaven and hell that was neither good nor bad, like a waiting room in forever, which, although obviously better than hell, still did not sound like much of a party at all. If we were very, very good, limbo was the best we could hope for. Our fate was sealed.

WE RELOCATED EVERY YEAR, like a family on the lam. Just when our mother had unpacked the dishware and settled us into our next primary school, my dad lifted his eyes to the horizon and chose the next destination. He was always unhappy, restless for one reason or another.

Our mother, with a career of her own and two small children, took this as a symptom of my father's desire to be baroquely difficult, or his maximalist's refusal to see the virtue in simplicity. Surgeons could also be famously temperamental, with unslaked ambitions and professionally itchy feet, always on the hunt for more than was realistically available. But itinerance was nothing new for my dad, whose home had been buried in the ash of memory, whose connection to the plains of Punjab was the stuff of wedding rituals and family yarns. By then he'd been living out of a figurative suitcase for nearly two decades.

At the hospital, my dad was the only Indian doctor, and his fortunes rose there about as much as they had in London. He spent a long time as an underdog, climbing the rungs, but waiting was never his forte. Nor was he meek or particularly compliant about it. By then he was showing up for work dressed like Henry Higgins, missing nothing in this costume of British doctorhood but a pipe, a watch fob, and a chain. He kept the beard but wore his hair short, if not to fit in, not exactly, then to avoid the costs of standing out. By all reports, he was a dedicated and competent surgeon. But just as in England, he seemed to be getting nowhere.

Despite the hope of a fresh North American start, the theme remained the same, what he perceived as Anglo-Saxon exceptionalism, merely transmuted across the pond. If the eastern outports left promises unfulfilled, then perhaps there was something better to be gained in the country's gravitational center. And so we moved yet again, for the fourth time in as many years, this time to Toronto.

Back then, Canada wasn't exactly a brown man's Valhalla, an observation made by the late author Bharati Mukherjee, who wrote a famously blistering essay titled "An Invisible Woman" in which she described the barrage of racial slurs and harassment she received upon moving to Toronto, including false accusations of shoplifting and demands she go "back to Africa." By the time the essay was published in 1981, Mukherjee had already decamped to San Francisco.

In the mid-seventies, Toronto was no rainbow utopia for my dad, either. Our family moved not to Coxwell and Gerrard, nor to Brampton, nor to any other of the immigrant enclaves, but to a house with a stone façade and a broad driveway where my dad could park his white Mercedes with pride—a used one, the first of several in his car-owning career, but a Mercedes nonetheless. Etobicoke, a borough on the western edge of the city, must have impressed him from afar with its imperial-sounding street names. It must have offered the subliminal comforts of England to my mother as well. The hospitals where they worked were named after saints, our schools after the knighted swashbucklers of a dying empire.

They'd also chosen an all-white neighborhood, not knowing any better, because it was close to work. Nobody brought them welcome cookies or invited them over for barbecues. Nobody wanted their kids to play with my brother and me, either. We learned to say "fucking asshole" on the kindergarten playground. In first grade, on our unaccompanied walk to school, we were intercepted by a gang of older kids who made us kneel down and kiss the ground beneath our feet—a gesture rich with unwitting irony.

But soon enough we turned the page once again. We began our next education in America.

WHAT  ARE YOU?

OUR PARENTS DECIDED ON THE UNITED STATES, THE Elysian Fields of the immigrant imagination, the palace in the sunset sky. What could be more hopeful than a nation of might and influence, the home of the Kennedys and space flight and California sunshine, a place where two decent jobs and free public schools weren't too much to ask for?

Our new town was a sleepy hamlet, nothing at all like Toronto. It lay north of Poughkeepsie and Schenectady and even Lake Placid, about as far as you could travel from New York City yet still remain within the Empire State. This county looked like a movie location, the kind of grassy upstate backwater where mafiosos go to lie low or farmers named Roscoe drive tractors across the unyielding land.

We moved onto a street named after a bird, but the bird's name was misspelled at every intersection, much to the dismay of our mother, who was a grammar purist. She sighed whenever she drove past *Nightengale* on the signage, at least for a little while, until the glitch became a normalized error, just another quirk of the landscape. But the problem remained for the entirety of our tumultuous decade in that house. When listing our address on immigration documents or school-enrollment forms, did one correct the error or duplicate it for fear of misdirection?

Perhaps our parents had learned a lesson from Toronto about prestigious suburbs and the perils of standing out. They bought a bland, medium-sized house in a medium-nice neighborhood. It had little curb appeal, was inoffensive and unshowy, with gray vinyl siding. It had white quartz chips beneath the foundation shrubbery, which was rangy and indestructible, a selling feature since no one watered or gardened in our household, save the occasional mowing. Out of public view, the backyard soon became infested in summer with tall dandelions, and our mother waged war with noxious dustings of weed killer, which we tracked into the house like baby powder on the soles of our bare feet.

Yellow carpet in the upstairs bathroom. Yankee-themed wallpaper in the downstairs powder room with a fife-and-drum motif. A few unremarkable bedrooms on the upper floor for us kids. An expansive main bedroom at the back of the house with a walk-in closet for our dad and a quiet, shady aspect for our mother—sleeping, along with secret church, had become her sacrament. The basement was creepy and unfinished, laced with spiderwebs and dust. Sometimes when it rained heavily, this subterranean level would flood, requiring onslaughts with a Shop-Vac and towels. The attic was insulated with fluffy shreds of asbestos vermiculite that I liked to make into wigs. With its trapdoor

and a fold-down ladder, it was also a good place to hide out
from our father if he was in unfavorable spirits.

We lived a stone's throw from the St. Lawrence, a mighty
waterway conveying the effluent of Lake Ontario, plus its
own discharge contributed by the many industries that lined
its shores. The riverbank was also home to the village beach,
where my brother and I swam and splashed and tried to
drown each other all summer long, just like the rest of the
local kids, who refused to get out until hypothermia set in.
Our mother swam here, too, in long breaststrokes along the
outer buoys; as a child she'd learned to swim in a chilly English sea. Everyone immersed in these semi-turbid waters except our dad, who found it insultingly cold. If he came to the
beach at all, he hung back on the brown sand, seldom ven-
turing in beyond his waist, looking perturbed about being
left behind. Despite knowing how to suture an incision with
the skill of a master tailor, he had never really learned how
to swim, we suspected.

Our new community glowed in the twilight of a fading
industrial boom. Many residents owed their rent and gro-
ceries to the automaking factory or the aluminum smelters
that chugged away on the edge of town. It was a strange
place for a family like ours to settle, as if we'd been guided
by a dart tossed randomly at a map. But both our parents
had found good jobs in these healthcare outlands and were
therefore indirectly employed by the factories as well. And
my dad, soured on Anglo Canada, was happy to have arrived in America, where the president was Jimmy Carter, a
peanut farmer with anti-segregationist leanings who'd forgiven draft dodgers for their wartime evasions. We owed at
least some of our luck to Senator Philip A. Hart of Michigan
and Emanuel Celler, a congressman from New York, whose

bill had opened the doors for millions of Asian immigrants and their families, most of whom had been previously barred from entry. In 1965, just nine years before our arrival, the quota system had been undone.

In summer our new world was a dream of sun and green leaves, the air filled with birds, buzzing insects, and lazily waving American flags. In winter the temperatures plunged, cloaking us all in a blanket of white, glittery powder, deepening as the days passed into a ritual of shoveling and snowblowing, the big plows banking it high in the streets, the feeble sun throwing its blue shadows. Here, life was a short walk to school in misty puffs of breath, with none of the dog-eat-dog of the city. There were no traffic jams, and cars lurked slowly down the streets since children roamed everywhere with unsupervised abandon. No one seemed too worried about anything. Everyone knew everyone else, or knew their business, at any rate. If people took umbrage at the racial disparities between our parents, or their in-between mocha children, nobody mentioned it. We moved in, and the neighborhood accepted us, or mostly accepted us, without a word of dissent, a development my dad seemed to relax into without surprise, as if he'd been expecting it all along.

Our mother was more gun-shy, slower to make friends. She remembered the polite hostilities of previous white neighborhoods. She'd never known these situations until she'd met our father, and they still had the power to surprise her. This time, she suspected the next-door neighbors who, despite having children of their own, tolerated us in stony silence. The vibe emanated mainly from the father, whose attitude was expressed in a sergeant-like demeanor and the militant maintenance of the perimeter shrubs between the two properties. Perhaps they disliked our stray Wiffle balls, or the ill-pegged underwear blown from the clothesline on our side over to theirs. Our garage door was always open, disgorging landslides of toys, softball mitts, bikes. But they were also a reclusive clan, with translucently indoor complexions—and surely, as with any family, problems of their own. Anyway, there was no way to tell the source of anyone's hostility. Did they not like *our kind,* or did they simply dislike us?

Historically, the region had been a dairy-farming community. It still was beyond the village limits, with rolling pastures, slumping barns, and bales of silage dotting the fields. In the 1800s, it had a famed sulfur spring whose eggy, healing waters attracted people like Theodore Roosevelt. But the medicinal spas and fancy hotels were gone, long since replaced by modern amenities: a liquor store, a donut shop, and a neglected park with splintery playground equipment. Upstream on the big river, a millionaire New York hotelier had built an imitation Rhineland castle, complete with 120 rooms and a drawbridge, in honor of his wife—or half-built, since construction was abandoned when she died. At the time of our first family visit, the castle was a sad tourist oddity, a weathered ruin, a caution against the dangers of outsized dreams and obscene wealth. Its rooms were graffitied with spray paint and smelled of pee in the corners.

A little later in the story, in the early parts of the twentieth century, upstate New York had been practically flooded with immigrants from Europe and Quebec, most of whom came to work in the factories at their operational zenith. By the time we showed up, there were still plenty of people with French-Canadian surnames, and many families whose Italian forebears had sailed from the old country. These olive-skinned newcomers had once suffered their own slings and arrows beyond the gates of Ellis Island, where the populace was largely white and Protestant. They'd been called lazy, swarthy, criminal, a whole host of slurs. But by the time we arrived they were thought of as normal Americans. My mother loved the resultant Catholic abundance. There were several churches and many masses to choose from throughout the week, to attend while my father wasn't paying attention.

Very few Jewish families lived among us, possibly due to an anti-Semitic incident that had occurred fifty years before. A four-year-old girl, lost while wandering in the woods, was rumored to have been abducted by local Jewish residents for the purposes of human sacrifice, resulting in a frenzy among the townsfolk, the police, and even the mayor. That's how our town claimed the dubious distinction of hosting America's one and only case of blood libel. But by the time we rolled in, no one ever mentioned that dark chapter. It had been forgotten, bleached from memory like a Polaroid in reverse.

There weren't many Black or brown households, either, and definitely nobody in a turban. Many of those families were healthcare imports as well, moving through on the way to elsewhere. An Indian husband with a Caucasian wife was an amusing curiosity more than a lurking threat to the neatened order of this self-contained universe. In a small town, who could argue with more healthcare?

It was a time of glorious oblivion. My parents rarely entertained, but when they did, guests smoked freely in our house, snuffing their cigarettes in a heavy glass ashtray kept expressly in the living room for their use. Some of the smokers were doctors. You could drive without wearing a seatbelt. You could bike without a helmet. You could ride without child seats, as we often did, sleeping in the back of our mother's station wagon on long trips. There was only one can for the garbage. No one knew about fat-free yogurt or doubted iceberg as an acceptable form of lettuce. It was a time of carefree abandon when you could say almost any old thing that came to mind. When people used racial epithets to describe their fellow humans, they did so right out in the open without any pause or embarrassment, without glancing over their shoulders to see who was around. Often they did so without apparent judgment or malice—these were the words that sprang readily to mind, a language to which no one had ever objected. No one flinched, at least not outwardly.

Outrage was saved for skyrocketing interest rates and epic lineups at the gas station. There had not yet been a Gulf War. Not yet the twin towers. Iran, prerevolution, was still ruled by the shah. People remembered Eisenhower's visit to Tehran, when the streets of his motorcade route were lined with Persian carpets. Indira Gandhi would soon reclaim her post as prime minister of India. There was no AIDS. No war on terror. Not yet a Gipper in the Oval Office. The nemesis was communism, and the enemies were Russians, mysterious white people on the far side of the Iron Curtain.

These were the allures of a small American town. We rolled ourselves into the fabric of life, far from the pull of New York City, which everyone knew was a grimy crime-ridden dystopia, where muggings happened every minute on the subway. By contrast, our town was a little bastion of safety, cold in the winter, manure-scented in spring. You could ride a bike across town in twenty minutes or walk it in an hour. We could dial local numbers using just five digits.

Nobody locked their front doors, and sometimes the locals, including our dad's patients and our babysitter's boyfriends, would just let themselves in without ringing the doorbell, before calling out their hellos. Nobody took off their shoes at the threshold. We lived in a style of oblivious innocence. We forgave and we forgot. Mostly it felt like a back pocket of America where ethnicity was the stuff of foreign films, unfolding distantly in crowded metropolises. Melting pots were where the aluminum was smelted. We were far from anywhere, now virtually untouched by the far-flung worlds from which we'd come. We were now part of a way of being, a mode of believing that enveloped us all, thick as a dump of snow.

CHARLOTTE AND ALEX, Alex and Charlotte. In our new American primary school, my brother and I were separated for the first time. Twins should not be together in the classroom, they said. It would delay our intellectual and psychological development. It was just the policy, they said. I was unused to hearing my name uttered all by itself. I'd seldom moved through space on my own, unaffected by my brother's pace, without hurrying to catch up or waiting for him to zip his coat or tie his shoes.

Whenever an adult raised their voice, or had hiccups, or had toilet paper stuck to the heel of their shoe—any stimulus at all that seemed unusual or funny or frightening— I would look to Alex to calibrate, knowing from his slightest frown or smirk how I should receive the situation. Without our repertoire of in-jokes and nonsense talk, I'd have to amuse myself or find my own friends, which felt like an unfair severance to me, in the second grade, for the very first time alone.

We were seven years old and then eight. Each morning we stood up in our classrooms and pledged allegiance to the Stars and Stripes. We said the Lord's Prayer whenever divine intervention was sought, before sporting events, for instance. I learned to recite this prayer by rote even though I had never spent any time inside a church. Our school staged duck-and-cover drills on the regular, and when the alarm sounded, we crouched beneath our desks and waited for the danger to pass. The danger was bomb threats, the Russians, the Cold War. These drills raised endless questions. For instance, how could our tiny desks, stuck with gum and chiseled by protractors, protect us from a nuclear explosion if it was a radiative tsunami capable of vaporizing everything in its path? And then, why would the enemy go to the trouble of nuking our little school, half a world away in an overlooked bumpkin town? These seemed like neurotically detailed schemes of mass destruction.

We called our teachers by their honorifics, never by their first names. Curriculum was standardized, but beyond the multiplication tables and cursive writing, our teachers were free to riff according to their interests. Social studies classes seemed especially prone to extemporaneous teaching. We watched black-and-white films about the defoliating menace posed by deer to local forests. Apparently, the rampant overpopulation of deer meant the need for culls, a community service provided by hunters, who were to be appreciated, as was the Second Amendment. But what if you identified with the deer?

It was a time of small divisions.

My parents went to work at two separate hospitals, our

mother administering her operating-room tranquilizers in the next town over, Dad doing his assembly line of cutting and suturing at the local general. Their schedules were all over the map, each of us set loose on our own daily trajectories. On rare nights when we ate dinner together, my parents engaged in a mystifying shoptalk to do with inflammatory conditions and ruptured internal body parts. This was our introduction to the morbid equalities of the body. No matter who you were, rich or poor, young or old, white, brown, or some other color—everyone wore the same old flesh suit.

"Why do people have to have their gallbladders removed?"

"Because they eat too many french fries," our mother replied. She was pregnant at the time and too tired to explain the science behind this organ's proper function, or the effects of diet on the liver, so for a long time I did not generalize the negative effects of too much dietary fat. I hung on to my suspicion of french fries, despite eating them in abundance, believing they possessed the singular power to send a person into an eventual health emergency. It mystified me that a natural-born organ could simply be removed, its function optional, without serious consequences to the owner. And what happened to this spongy, unwanted tissue once it had been taken out? Where did it go?

Why?

Why?

Why?

Our father often became testy, especially at the dinner table. He did not like the way kids sucked up everyone's attention, the way they derailed adult conversation. He did not like the gibberish of twinship, nor the secret nonsense jokes, nor our silliest joys. He didn't appreciate the way our mother seemed to enjoy it all, or at least permit it without much comment or correction. At the end of a hard day, he disliked noise, sibling disharmony, unanswered telephones, theatrical crying, and most kinds of domestic malfunction, even if these were the forces that seemed to rule our days. To him, a house was a world of trickle-down entitlements; those were the rules that he'd known. He did not like it when the household revolved around the littlest people, the rightful pyramid flipped upside-down. But most of all, he was envious of our mother's love for us, which was effort-less, unconditional, formed in the blood.

Then our little sister arrived, the first natural-born North American. Alex was the darkest and most Indian-looking. I was a close second, in the middle of our pigment gradient. But she was the whitest child, as our mother liked to joke, as if the ink had run out at the printer. My sister, with her fair skin and hazel eyes, was also my dad's favorite, virtually from birth. She looked most like our mother in complexion, but she was most like him in temperament. She had a highly selective appetite and, for the first several years of life, sur-vived on a diet of saltines and pepperoni. She taught herself to read, and rather than bash around outside with us, she preferred to sit in quiet corners turning pages.

Perhaps, for the briefest flicker, our parents had envi-sioned model European children, the kind who waited po-litely to be spoken to, who never put their elbows on the table, who were seen but never heard. The sort of mini-adults who arrive for dinner with freshly washed hands and combed hair, who say "please" and "thank you" without prompting. But alas, whatever their high hopes for us, they'd wilted on the drive across the border.

My brother spoke in mumbles. I talked in an incessant

stream-of-consciousness narration through every waking hour. We'd spent just enough time at our new elementary school to glean a hint of the behavioral possibilities. Snot was hilarious, as were burps, intestinal gas, and the half-chewed contents of our mouths. If you didn't feel like doing the spelling test, you could glue your fingers together with Elmer's, and nobody would think to stop you. We seized these golden opportunities with both hands.

Our mother and father diverged in their parenting styles, but the crassness of North American child-rearing shocked them both equally. People let their offspring eat dinner on the floor in front of the TV. Kids were allowed to monopolize the telephone, and they were given their own bedrooms, which then descended into ungrateful squalor. Report cards came and went like grocery-store flyers, put out in the trash without a second glance. Our parents disagreed about many things, but they united in the worry we'd grow up into grass-stained chimps with twangy accents, bubble-gum breath, and a poor grasp of math and table manners—not far from what actually happened.

My twin and I were violently exuberant kids, fueled on a newfound cornucopia of American junk food. We expressed our energy through physical means, wrestling and even brawling whenever sibling rivalry demanded it. All through the house the drywall was pocked with doorknob holes because that's what we did. We destroyed things. We were doctors' children, with no respect for delicacy, or the hard-won cost of nice things. We gravitated toward fragile objects with a hungry sense of demolition, proving early on that our parents' taste for slender-legged antiques and cream-colored upholstery had been a terrible idea.

My brother and I shared a deep love of processed food

and fizzy beverages, which was also our father's weakness. Together we raided his private reserves of Coke and imported Jaffa Cakes in the after-school hours before he returned from work, knowing very well it would send him into a fury. Our mitochondria burned on Pop-Tarts and Big Wheels. Jungle Juice ran through our veins. Our mother bought these things for us despite her preference for the rustic foods of the old country. Her affection for whole-grain bread, hard-boiled eggs, and plain yogurt was trumped by our aversion to fiber and crunchy vegetables, but also by her faith in science, and therefore the foods made by science for harried moms, including Instant Breakfast, Tuna Helper, and Snack Mate spray cheese, delivered straight from canister to mouth.

My siblings and I became intimately familiar with the chalky terrors of Carnation instant powdered milk, whose bluish translucence and lurking clumps both haunted and fascinated us. The irony of this reconstituted-dairy phase was not lost on us, considering we lived in upstate New York; there were actual milk cows everywhere, dotting the rolling green hills, just like the illustrations on cans of evaporated milk. So close, yet so far from our Frosted Mini-Wheats.

Our mother loved those red cardboard boxes of granulated dairy because they never expired, the supply could be buttressed during a sale, and they didn't require last-minute trips to the grocery store or the management of perishable inventory. Powdered milk was a precious inch of reclaimed cognitive overhead.

My brother and I were huge fans of Swanson dinners, which we adored for their compartmentalized servings of mashed potatoes and chocolate pudding cake. Our mother loved these as well because they could be bought in a convenient stack of assorted flavors and stored in the freezer until the nuclear apocalypse. She didn't overthink food or worry about our nutrition, and in a way, this was totally freeing for everyone. Eating was not like a sacrament or a painful chore, but something fun, something within our power and control when most things beneath my father's roof were not.

To us, America was all-abundant. We embraced its vulgar patois, a foreign language as far as our parents were concerned, a code of repellent grunts sprinkled with mystifying pop-culture references. We wore polyester baseball jerseys and Tang-stained T-shirts, Nikes and roller skates, which I wasn't above using inside the house if our dad was out, since the main floor was laid out in a loop like a little racetrack: hallway to kitchen to dining room to living room and back again to the hallway, with enlivening speed bumps where the floor transitioned from linoleum to carpet.

It took no time at all for us to fall in with a gang of free-range kids from the neighborhood. In the summer, we raced our bikes up and down the streets and wandered into the woods to light little fires. We relied on no one to take us anywhere, not even to school, nor to approve the adequacies of our outerwear, even in the bitter cold of winter. We had a different mental map than the one our parents understood; ours was marked by friends' houses, convenience stores, and the homes of suspected perverts. We ran where we wanted to go, cutting through side yards and pruned bushes. We careened all over town and beyond, our wheels spinning, the loose dogs nipping at our heels, the wind roaring in our ears, with purloined change from our father's pockets. We spun through this part of our childhood, our mouths stained by Bomb Pops and dusted with powdered sugar. We hurled ourselves into the maw of American life and let it digest us whole.

THIRD GRADE, AND then the fourth. We staged mock elections during the presidential race of 1980, the year of the first Reagan-Bush victory. By then Carter had become the stagflation president, a kiss of death in a blue-collar town, as inept with the economy as with foreign threats. Nobody in my household possessed the right to vote, but I cast mine for Carter-Mondale anyway, joined by a tiny minority of anonymous lefties—the nerds, the weaklings, the kids with vegetarian, no-nukes moms. We lost by a landslide, much to the delight of our teacher, Mrs. Taylor, whose shellacked dome of flaxen curls reminded me of my grandmother's.

We had classroom visits from guests in uniform, sheriffs and state troopers who came to educate us about the dangers of juvenile criminality. They loomed before our chalkboards with their broad-brimmed hats and fascinating holstered guns to relate cautionary tales about the junior arsonists and larcenists they'd encountered in their careers. In these stories, delinquency had its roots in negligent, hippie parenting. It was also born of poverty, and poverty arose from squalor, a condition that could be remedied with vigorous hygiene. Soap was cheap, just pennies a bar. There was no excuse for filth, just as there was no excuse for going to jail. All these things fit together. Ivory Snow, goodness, and the purity of being American.

In the later years of my public-school education, we'd go on field trips to the county courthouse and jail, where the bars clanked open and shut for our educational benefit.

We'd spend lavish amounts of time on American history, government, and the Constitution, which was described as a sacred document, like the tablets of Moses brought down from the mount. We were taught an abbreviated history of the world, which to me seemed all but cleansed of its most interesting parts. Sure, we learned about battles and conquests, kings and princes, but what did the people eat for lunch if not leftover frozen pizza? How did they take baths with no running water? Where did the girls go to school?

We began not with the Celts, the barbarians, or any of the illiterate tribes of ancient, blue-eyed Europe, but with the Magna Carta, as if civilized democratic society had sprung forth spontaneously from English soil. Our lessons whisked us through the Middle Ages, favoring an encyclopedic survey of dates over the detailed specters of the Black Death, the Crusades, and the Spanish Inquisition. The violent campaigns of Europe were presumably too dark for children's consumption. After that, history seemed almost exclusively populated by men in breeches and powdered wigs, if you didn't count the royal women who featured as queens and princesses in dynastic intermarriages.

We spent a long time on the Protestant Reformation and the Age of Discovery. But we learned virtually nothing about Africa and Asia beyond the nations that had conquered them, as if these were shadow continents, waiting in benighted dormancy for the sailing ships to arrive. We learned all about the Puritans and the *Mayflower*. On our quizzes we were asked to align each seaboard state with its colonial origins. New York was a debtor colony. Virginia was a cotton and tobacco colony. We learned about the transatlantic slave trade as if through an interstellar telescope, as if it was a precondition to the abolitionist movement and the Civil War. But nothing of its visceral truths, at least not from the point of view of enslaved people.

Our town sat adjacent to a large Kanien'kehá:ka reservation, and many of the children from that community attended public school with us. They learned about their own ancestors, their very own tribes, as if they were disappeared figments from the past. We learned about Jim Crow, too, but not in any serious or impactful detail, as if these laws were mere administrative relics governing the function of water fountains and entrance signage.

I took my share of Scantron exams, the ones with the empty ovals that you fill in with a pencil. I grew to dislike them, but not for the usual reasons—the performance anxieties, the ticking clocks, the long rows of desks lined up in the gym, or even the prospect of my father scrutinizing my results.

The exam booklets always had a section devoted to the harvest of personal and statistical information where I'd find this question: *What is your racial background?* Always the same one, or versions of it, followed by a list of acceptably compartmentalized ethnic groups: white, Black, Asian, etc. I couldn't reply accurately because only one response was allowed, and I didn't have just one answer. I looked around at my mostly white classmates and felt confused, but there was no box for that. So, I usually just checked "Other," which at the time felt about right.

I had no idea what pigeonhole to choose. "Asian" seemed big, like the broad side of a barn. I didn't feel particularly Indian, even though my brother and I looked like my dad, undeniably so. His traits were dominant, our mother's recessive. In keeping with their personalities, his features showed

up at the forefront, whereas hers lay beneath in the architec-
ture, in the structure of our bones and faces. In the parental
donation of physical traits, our father had won by a landslide, but I couldn't discriminate. I accepted the mismatch of
their physical features as idiosyncrasies, the matter of skin
being no more important than the shape of a nose or the
length of one's fingers. I didn't perceive the value, the meaning of the difference between them, nor the shade variega-
tion I shared with my brother. I couldn't see how this space
might widen over time, so that one day they'd no longer
belong to each other, and as their children, we'd cease to be
the sum of their parts, not as we'd been in the beginning,
before we grew into a middle zone that only we could feel
and understand.

In the midst of this early education, I tried hard to think
of myself as normal and regular, just like any other kid in
class. Ivory Snow, American purity, etc. But I knew it was
impossible. My dad was Indian. My mom was English. They
had accents and used all the wrong names for things. Our
village was ruled by working-class sensibilities, and few men
wore suits, my dad excluded. As soon as he hit America, he
doubled down on the fashion, as if he'd raided the wardrobe
department of *Saturday Night Fever*. My mother, on the
other hand, talked like she'd come from a place where people still wore chain mail and ermine robes. She was nothing
like the other moms with their long nails and Virginia Slims,
their feathered hair and Jordache jeans.

I dressed in cowboy shirts and corduroys and sneakers.
These were my clothes, what I'd always worn, but they were
also the disguise of North America, chosen for maximum
camouflage. I did whatever I could to sneak through, to
show I was just like everyone else. But my classmates saw

right through me. They knew precisely what questions to ask, almost right from the start. Why did I have dark circles around my eyes? Why were my lips purple and not pink? That's how I began to see myself through other people's eyes, not only in the first person, but also in the third.

My mother was no accurate mirror, either. She never mentioned skin tone or race—not hers, ours, or our father's. "I only saw you as mine," she says even now. Our father seldom discussed it, either, just like he never talked about Kenya, his youth, or any part of his life before medical school. All roads led back to Africa and my grandparents, who never called or sent cards or gifts in the mail, at least none that I ever saw, whose silence was total and adamant.

GOODBYE, 6 MOTHERLAND

IN THE 1930S, WHEN INDIA WAS STILL A JEWEL IN THE crown, my paternal grandfather left his village in the Punjab for Kenya. He was just a teenager. He made this trip alone after the death of his mother, my great-grandmother. He was still a boy, but he'd already become a man.

My grandfather built a life for himself in Nairobi before going back to India, where he married my grandmother. Then they returned to Africa. The order of those events shifts and changes depending on who in the family retells the story, but no matter the version, one thing remains true. Ever since that first departure, my paternal family, along with my own nuclear unit, has been on the move.

My father was born in India but grew up in Kenya, and when he came of age, my grandfather approved the idea of medical school in London. My dad went back to Kenya a couple of times after med school, but he knew his future lay elsewhere. He never returned to Punjab, either. In fact, I have spent more time in India than he has, despite the fact that he was born there, and for quite a while carried an Indian passport.

If India had never been a British colony, I doubt my grandfather would have left his natal village. If Kenya wasn't also a colony in need of subordinate staffing, my grandfather might not have ventured there to begin with. And if England wasn't considered the educational apex of the Empire, I doubt my father would have gone there at all. But to be honest, I don't know why my grandfather decided to pack up and ship out in the first place. I never got the chance to ask.

According to my dad, my grandfather left home without any family. But he was far from alone in his travels. Many Indians came this way, young and unaccompanied. He sailed in a dhow, a ship with an ancient design, its rigging expressly suited to the trade winds of the Indian Ocean. These winds blew from northeast to southeast in winter, and in the opposite direction in summer, a handy circle from northern Indian seaports to Africa and back again. Arabs, Persians, Indians, and traders from the Far East had been plying these waters for centuries, bringing implements and furnishings, textiles, perfumes, and weaponry in exchange for gold, ivory, rhinoceros horns, dye, and timber.

By the latter half of the nineteenth century, the British had also cottoned to East Africa's riches. Kenya offered agricultural possibilities, a favorable tropical climate, and large tracts of land—open for the taking if one overlooked the current occupants. Conversely, India was seen by the British as an "overpopulated" country weakened by famine, with a population ripe for emigration to its sister colony in East Africa, where Indians might function as obedient lackeys to the Crown. After all, Indians had grown accustomed to the habits and predilections of Anglos after generations of living beneath the viceroys.

The great Maasai spiritual leader Mbatian prophesied the occupation of his homelands in a vision of an iron snake. As with so many colonial incursions, this manifested as a railway built from the coast into the kingdom of Buganda, refashioned by the British into the Uganda Protectorate, which was landlocked behind Kenya but nevertheless promised further economic opportunities in the form of untapped mineral deposits, forest resources, and cash-crop potential. The Uganda Railway widened immigration channels between India and Kenya, where some thirty-two thousand Indians would find work at the turn of the nineteenth century in the direct business of laboring or making trade with those who did. By the time the project was done, nearly ten thousand people had died or been gravely injured.

After the railway's completion at the turn of the century, all kinds of people began showing up in Kenya, many seeking to capitalize on the space made by colonialism and its long reach into previously inaccessible corners. After the railway, Indian immigrants, mostly from the north, plied a diversity of trades. They were artisans, merchants, and tradespeople, domestic staff and the hired administrative hands of the colonial bureaucracy. My grandfather was part of that wave.

The city of Nairobi had once been a whistle-stop on the way to Mombasa, but it developed into the administrative heart of British East Africa. It was a home away for the Anglo bureaucrats stationed there, and for private citizens lured by the attractions of the colony, which included better weather, more room, and sufficient amounts of equatorial indolence, since Kenya was perceived, at least for whites, as an "overseer's country." Some of these expats were self-exiled aristocrats who'd run afoul of reputation back at home, or they sought the sort of hedonic fantasyland detailed in the work of Karen Blixen, whose memoir, *Out of Africa,* described her life in Kenya. Blixen lived there from 1914 to 1931, and in that time her Kenyan staff cooked and carried for her, attending to her every need. Her bathwater was fetched by hand when she went on safari, and her favorite shotgun was toted by an attendant whose singular job that was. Blixen also ran a farm with labor provided by Kikuyu "servants," who worked to pay tax to British governors, in effect indenturing them on their own lands. In the Kenyan highlands just outside Nairobi, the Happy Valley set, a clique of wealthy European and American expats, lived an orgiastic lifestyle fueled by booze, opiates, and the toil of yet more Kikuyu laborers, plenty of whom lived in shacks on their masters' properties.

Nairobi grew into a place with bars, billiards halls, and hotels catering to big-game hunters from Europe. It was a playground for elites and rogues alike with its racetracks and polo grounds. At the Muthaiga Country Club, the clientele drank champagne for breakfast, and English barons rode their horses right into the Norfolk Hotel for spontaneous bouts of steeplechase. Terrible fun, but only if you were rich and white, since these were deeply segregated spaces. Local Kenyans, despite being the largest demographic in the city, could only reside in Nairobi as registered workers. Indian immigrants were forbidden from owning farmland. Both groups were barred from entering "public" facilities frequented by the British. This is the place where my grandfather lived, or rather, the world he lived beside. It's where he built a furniture-making business, selling his wares to the British.

My grandfather was a smart man. That's what everyone says. By the time his household was full of children, he was no longer the same person who'd left Punjab. He was the head of his own clan, the maker of his own fortune, respected, formidable, and often fearsome. In photos, he has light skin compared to many in our family, a long nose, a thick white beard, and a trim, low-riding turban. He's often wearing a suit jacket and a plain white shirt. No tie, no bling, no flaming colors. He was known to carry a gun around on his rambles through Nairobi. According to family lore, this weapon lived in a safe atop stacks of cash, but the resemblance of this image to a Hollywood trope gives me just a little pause. Apparently, he also owned a gin still. In addition to furniture, he made the Englishman's favorite spirit, but I don't know if that's true. In my experience, gin is not the poison of choice for Sikh men, if they drink at all. It's whiskey. My dad tells me that his father knew Barack Obama, Sr., but that could be apocryphal, too.

I don't know exactly what's true because we spent many years out of contact with our kin, no matter our curiosity or private yearning for the aunts, uncles, and cousin-playmates we knew populated the unknown side of the tree. Our dad's side was big and sprawling, while our mother's was small and tight, devoted, as they'd always been, to life in jolly old England. By a twist of colonial irony, most of my dad's sisters would eventually settle there, too, once they left home to marry abroad—appropriately, to the right Indian suitors, with my grandfather's blessings.

As the people out on the ice floe, we attended not one Sangeet or Anand Karaj. I doubt we received many invitations, either. Most of our relatives knew better than to extend an olive branch behind my grandfather's back. He was the uber-patriarch, and his wish was almost everyone's command. Our mother had no idea what we might be missing, either. She'd never set foot inside a Sikh temple.

For decades, my father was persona non grata, or so he tells me now. Back then he avoided my grandfather with a kind of reverence, skirting the mere mention of his name, as if tiptoeing around a curse. My dad isn't one to express open guilt, or to use the words "shame" or "sorry." But his parents' culture was deeply concerned with the artifacts of prediasporic custom, with honor—possibly more old-world, by the late twentieth century, than the villages from which they'd come. From their point of view, the family had been forced to wear my father's transgressions. He'd married a white lady, humiliated his folks, absconded to America, and then would eventually, inevitably, blight the very union that had tarnished the family honor in the first place. That's what we'd become before the decade was out, a broken family within a broken family, as if that were a rare or world-ending affliction.

When I was a child, family news filtered down to us through our father's sister in Texas, who lived far enough away from the old man to get away with it. We knew who had gotten married and who had moved house or had babies. I'd never met our grandparents, had never talked to them on the phone. We didn't speak their language. But I inferred that our grandfather was strong, even stubborn, in his beliefs. His adherence to tradition was legendary, despite the tattoos on his forearms—a naked woman on one side, a pistol on the other—which he concealed beneath long sleeves, a telltale of wilder times. No matter his country of residence, he carried a torch for the old ways as if they were endangered phenomena, which perhaps in some ways they were. These governed an old-school Sikh's responsibilities and all his relations, how he spent money, who his children could marry, the men he could befriend, the people he talked to in the street. We were the outcasts in the West, where everyone on my dad's side seemed to want to venture for the sake of a better life, but not totally, not if the excesses of a Western lifestyle came with it.

My grandfather finally agreed to see my dad again, but not until decades had passed, and he was close to the age my father is now. Maybe this was less about forgiveness than it was the acquiescence of an old man who knew he was close to the end. It seemed like an unyielding way to be, but we didn't know his heart. I didn't know his history, the places he'd come from, all that he'd seen and done.

MATCHMAKING, IN MY grandparents' youth, was arranged through word of mouth across kinship networks. Tinder was literally the stuff used to start a cooking fire. If a family wished to find a bride for their son, the range of eligible girls might be discovered within a long day's walk, about the distance between my grandparents' villages, which lay a hundred miles east, as the crow flies, from what is now the Pakistan border. My grandmother was still a child at the time of her nuptials, sixteen when my dad was born. This was just ten years before the sectarian carnage of Partition began. Maybe my grandfather smelled a bad smoke coming on the wind, because that's when they returned to Africa.

Punjab is split between two countries today, India and Pakistan. But in my grandfather's youth, and my dad's early years as well, it was one continuous territory, with people from multiple ethnoreligious groups living side by side, as they'd done for centuries. For my grandmother, it couldn't have been easy to uproot. Her people, who were also my grandfather's kind, had lived in Punjab for so long it must have seemed like forever. But their clan, the Jats, had been arrivals themselves, pastoral nomads who'd moved in from arid regions to the south during the Middle Ages. They'd settled down to lives of subsistence farming and become, over time, politically and economically dominant in Punjab despite their minority population in that state.

Punjab is, and has always been, a prized breadbasket. It's also situated in the path of one of the most storied geopolitical bottlenecks in the world, the Khyber Pass, the funnel through which countless armies have poured onto the subcontinent from parts north and west. Punjab has been ruled by Afghans, three Turkish dynasties, the Mongols, then more Afghan governors. Then, for over two centuries, it was part of the Mughal empire.

In many ways the story of Punjab is one of watchfulness. The dramatis personae are poor farmers stooped in the fields, their eyes flicking to the west as they wait for the next invaders to maraud down the mountainsides with swords rattling. All this hardscrabble living and perennial destruction lent a vigilant pride to the culture, what Indian historian Khushwant Singh once described as a "frontier consciousness," a survivor mentality that manifests as a certain "restive" disposition. This character runs almost entirely counter to the model-minority stereotype, in my experience anyway. I recognize its headstrong scrappiness very well. It's classically my dad, by coincidence or not.

Punjab spent many centuries as an occupied territory, its

people paying tribute to foreign sultanates, kings, queens, and viceroys. Sikhs experienced a brief period of self-sovereignty in the first half of the nineteenth century under the leadership of Ranjit Singh, otherwise known as the "Lion of Punjab." Singh was an illiterate pauper who became a maharaja, whose purported ugliness concealed humility, intelligence, and a knack for military strategy, which he deployed with careful ambition on behalf of his people. The Sikh Empire lasted just fifty years, but even in the midst of this heyday the British had already arrived; they conspired to expand their influence northward on the subcontinent. The Lion of Punjab was blind in one eye, but he foresaw that the Raj would eventually claim all of India, a reality that came to pass a mere decade after his death. When the Crown annexed Punjab in 1849, it was the last Indian province to fall to imperial rule.

A mere century later, the British could not flee India fast enough. The retreat of the Raj in 1947 set the stage for one of the largest mass migrations—and worst humanitarian disasters—the world has ever seen. The excision of Pakistan from India along religious lines—predominantly Hindus from Muslims—was preceded by months of political battling and escalating sectarian violence in cities throughout India. The withdrawal of the Empire was overseen by Lord Louis Mountbatten, the last viceroy of India, who shortened the countdown to handover by nearly a year, a move with disastrous consequences.

A new boundary was hastily fashioned, cleaving the Islamic State of Pakistan from India, by Cyril Radcliffe, a British judge who'd never been to India until called upon to redraw nearly 4,000 miles of border in just five weeks. Radcliffe quickly discovered the areas in question weren't just

real estate on a map but rather an old ethnoreligious patchwork of complexly intermingled communities that proved
nearly impossible to separate along clear, straight lines. But
by the time of independence, the job was done. Punjab and
Bengal were cut in half, and a great migration of refugees
began, a displacement that would eventually see some fifteen million people crossing from one side to the other
across a lawless, intensely volatile landscape.

Punjab became ground zero for much of the brutal,
bloody fallout. As the British withdrew their forces, armed
militias went from village to village, ransacking and pillag-
ing, abducting women and children, before setting whole
communities ablaze. Overflowing passenger trains were am-
bushed, and all their occupants slaughtered. Children were
forced to watch as their parents were tortured and executed.
Girls and women were savagely raped, their bodies branded
and mutilated.

Atrocities were committed on both sides in one of the
most vicious and terrorizing instances of ethnic cleansing in
human history. By the time the violence drew to a close, the
countryside was strewn with bodies, literally stained red
with blood. An unfathomable number had perished, up to
an estimated two million people. Two new nations had come
into being, free but devastated by the processes of decolonization and separation. The governments of both India and
Pakistan worked intensely to rise from those ashes, but Partition became a deep wound whose legacy is still felt today.

KENYA DECLARED INDEPENDENCE in 1963, and Asians were
issued an ultimatum: become Kenyan citizens or apply for a
British passport. Most Indians in Kenya chose the latter. It's

illuminating to me that my grandfather chose to stay. Perhaps it was preference, the old familial resistance, or maybe a little of both. But whatever nostalgia my grandparents may have felt for Punjab, their homeland had changed forever in the period of their absence, its map redrawn, its scars now running deep.

My grandparents stayed in Nairobi, the house empty of children, until declining health triggered their move to the United Kingdom in the wake of their daughters' relocation. It must have been a comfort to see tasseled khanda pendants hanging from rearview mirrors in the parking lots of Heathrow Airport, to spot the golden domes of gurdwaras in the London suburbs, where they'd eventually end up. To know there were people around them who were guided by the same deep undercurrent of spiritual life, no matter how much the scenery changed.

They followed the teachings of Sikhism, which trace back to the life of Guru Nanak, who originated the no-frills, one-god religion my dad still admires—even if he doesn't follow it to the letter. Guru Nanak, like Jesus, was a wandering prophet. He was born a Hindu in fifteenth-century Punjab, but one day he walked out of his house, leaving his wife and two sons behind, for a life of mendicant preaching. He rejected existing Hindu and Muslim scriptures and instead presented an idea of God as an abstract creator. He taught that spirituality was an inward experience, achievable through meditation, not wealth, status, or other material trappings, which presents me with quite the contrast when I think of my dad's predilections.

Nanak eschewed the rigid social segregations of his day. All people, men and women included, were equals before God—at least in theory. This egalitarian message was very

popular in medieval Punjab, especially among the lowborn
with no access to salvation under Hindu caste strictures. He
amassed a following of householders that included peasants
and slaves—the Jats among them.

After Nanak, the Sikh faith was carried and developed
by nine subsequent gurus, all of whom lived in times of Islamic rule. The first four sheltered beneath the reign of the
Mughal emperor Akbar, a relatively tolerant king. But
within months of Akbar's death from dysentery, Guru Arjan
Dev, the fifth guru, was executed by the new emperor. He
became the first Sikh martyr. The second martyr was Guru
Tegh Bahadur, the ninth in line, a dignified, intensely committed man of the faith who was a poet as well as a highly
trained warrior. He was beheaded in 1675 by Aurangzeb,
the sixth Mughal emperor, after refusing to convert to Islam.

At this point, the Sikhs had had enough. Guru Gobind
Singh, the tenth and final guru, was stabbed by assassins
and succumbed to his wounds in 1708. But before his death
he founded the Khalsa, an order of initiated Sikhs. That's
when the religion took on its martial overtones, its politi-
cized dream of a homeland, and its five identifying signs,
among them the turban and the ceremonial dagger.

For my grandparents, this was their bedrock, their foun-
dational story, a narrative tinged with sacrifice, pride, and a
fighting spirit, played out upon heated, contested soil. Its
message emphasized uprightness and dignity, even in the
face of persecution, with a countervailing softness in the
form of equality and charitable service. According to my
dad, in his lapsed religious state, it's still a "sensible philosophy of life."

Sometimes I can see in him, and in my family at large, the
outlines of Sikh temperament—if it's even fair to generalize

so crassly. This collection of traits is relatively easy to spot, in part because they stand out from Western ways, but also because I'm an outlier, at least partially. From my dad, I've learned there's modesty, even in miserable times. What's the point of lamenting one's losses and setbacks if misfortune, just like happiness, springs from a divine source, the will of God? Put on a brave face! Suffer in style! This emotional restraint aligned very well with the British stiff upper lip, which might be why my mother and father got along so well in the first place. Possibly it led to their downfall as well.

But regardless of what became of their union, my dad always faces forward. He seldom wallows or dwells in the past. His natural fallback position is upbeat, a skip in the step, in keeping, consciously or not, with the Sikh embrace of joy—a buoyant mental state in the face of adversity as a sign of submission to the will of God.

A QUESTION THAT often gets asked during interviews: Who would you invite to a dinner party, living or dead? You're supposed to name a legendary or celebrity figure, but I'd always choose my grandparents. They had many grandchildren, dozens in fact, so I'm not sure they would have felt the missed opportunity as keenly as I do.

I know my grandmother only from photos. Often in these pictures, she is surrounded by visiting grandkids, smiling with her head thrown back, eyes closed. She's a cardigan-wearing little person with toasted-almond skin, a dupatta draped over her head in the old-school way. I'm told she was a quietly joyful person, always retiring, mostly in the background. She'd received just a rudimentary education, never proceeding past primary school, typical for a traditional Indian girl in her day. She spoke little English. She was gentle and shy. But on the other hand, she was obsessed with pro wrestling. Any chance she got, she'd slip out of the kitchen to sit in front of the TV and shake her fist at "Macho Man" Randy Savage. She spent many a happy hour watching Hulk Hogan and the other greased, spray-tanned beefcakes of the World Wrestling Federation chokeslam and piledrive each other into the canvas. Such are the contradictions in my family.

When my dad was training to be a doctor in England, airfares weren't cheap. Sometimes he'd spend long, uninterrupted stretches without ever going home. My grandmother said her goodbyes to her firstborn son, knowing it might be many months before she saw him again, never imagining that it might be years, on just a few occasions, the last time near the end of her life. Now, when I ask my dad how she felt about all of this, he shrugs and looks away. She never said anything about it, he tells me, as per the usual ironclad stoicism.

"But how do you think she *felt*?" I ask.

"I think she was sad," he replies.

My grandmother passed first. She died of cancer. My grandfather lived until his late eighties. After they'd both gone, the family home remained there in Kenya, the suburbs grown up around it. It was rented out for many years and then eventually sold, cutting that family tether.

NATURALIZED CITIZENS

IT TOOK JUST A FEW YEARS OF UPSTATE, MIDDLE-CLASS living for us kids to assimilate, *almost*. But for my dad, the American Dream was a double-edged blade. He was the surgeon son of a Jat Sikh "industrialist," as my grandfather might have described himself back in the day, using the lingo of peak Indian success. But nobody knew about my dad's provenance, or was impressed by it, not in England, or Toronto, or even upstate New York. His dark complexion and thick accent made people think of an overpopulated country with open sewers and cows wandering about in the streets. Claw your way out of the bucket, fine. But beyond that, you could rule the Duchy of Cornwall and nobody would be impressed. Pedigree was for chumps, at least it was in our little blue-collar world, a reality he refused to take lying down.

In the land of debt and dreams, my mother never knew

what to do with luxury, not even when she could afford it. By the time the eighties rolled around, she'd bought a Toyota Tercel wagon with four-wheel drive and a clinometer on the dashboard. Hers was a philosophy of constant preparedness for heavy-tilt situations, no matter where they might present. This car was totally family-friendly; it fit one twin in the passenger's seat and one in the back, plus a car seat for our little sister until she outgrew it. Our mother's ark was built to fit her whole brood, to weather any storm.

For a little while, my father drove a Lincoln Town Car. When he sat behind the wheel it looked like a cross between a getaway vehicle and a self-driven limousine. After that, he bought a Corvette with a smoked-glass sunroof and a low-riding undercarriage entirely unsuited to our wintry northern conditions. My dad hated shoveling snow—that was our job. But when we neglected our duties, or if it snowed overnight, he put his foot down on the gas and gunned it in reverse until escape velocity was achieved. Sometimes it took a few tries before the Corvette could blast through the white berm in the street left behind by the municipal plow.

My brother and I transformed into gawky tweens with crooked smiles and overgrown mullets. Our little sister was now in kindergarten, an academic step back considering she'd begun reading at age three. As siblings, our lopsided reproductive spacing reflected the haphazardness of our parents' journey. Opportunities presented through serendipity and happenstance, if not exactly through practicality or long-term planning. These were seized in the moment and run down, then wrung out and lit on fire.

When we'd first moved in, the people of the village did double takes whenever we appeared together in public, but after a handful of years in the gray vinyl house, they just got used to the oddball multi-toned family down the road. With no threat of relocation looming on the horizon, our mother settled in. She was free to indulge in her many savings regimes. She couldn't throw anything out. Twist ties, bread tags, empty baby food jars. It wasn't unusual to open the fridge and find leftovers packed in surgical implement trays she'd salvaged from the operating room. She mailed Christmas presents to our cousins packed not with tissue paper but with foam cutouts shaped like artificial hip joints.

When it came to fiscal restraint, she was the Hoover Dam compared to our dad's Niagara. Money stretched further than it did in the city, an unforeseen benefit for a brown cosmopolitan man with good taste. There was at least one restaurant with white tablecloths, and although all he could expect were amuse-bouches of pimento-stuffed olives and cottage cheese, we went there often, usually as a family. He went without us, too, on nights when he didn't like the look of the weeknight casserole bubbling away in the oven. But it was hard to know for sure how he spent his cash since his Achilles' heel was wining and dining, plus a semisecret penchant for hotels and airline tickets, as we'd all discover later on. These left no trace after they'd been experienced, nothing at all to show for the expense. This was also the beginning of his fascination with media technology. We got a Sony TV with digital buttons instead of an analog dial, then a VCR, which we weren't allowed to touch, even though we were the only ones who knew how to operate it.

These were contradictory times. The Iran hostage crisis appeared on the news like a strange and hyper-real thriller, and then John Lennon died. The nation was bogged down by high unemployment and 18 percent mortgages. Lady Di got married in a torrential froth of taffeta and old lace. Kids everywhere zipped around their Pac-Man mazes, gobbling power pellets.

My parents loved modern science and invention, but at the same time, our contemporary era confused them. They'd been born in an epoch when gas cost nineteen cents a gallon and women wore girdles. In the United Kingdom they'd left behind, ballerinas were the only people dancercising in leotards, and shoulder pads were protective gear worn for uncouth body-contact sports. Our parents had come to the West to reap its benefits but recoiled from its many vulgarities. And yet this cultural mood was the one that most coincided with my dad's over-the-top sensibilities.

Even our thrifty mother got caught in her own consumer conundrum. She loved time-saving domestic gadgetry. My dad did not perform household chores, literally did not know how, and if he was pushed to it by circumstance, the results were usually worse than the original muss. Appliances liberated her sentient hours. She bought a portable dishwasher that rolled across the floor and attached with a hose to the kitchen faucet. Then she bought a microwave, a coffin-sized wonder of technology that took up all the real estate on one kitchen counter. This device democratized meals since anyone, even our father, could pull a frozen puck from the freezer and place it inside, usually without a plate, and watch it bubble, puff up, and transform into food, or a food-like facsimile. Why learn to cook when we could press our foreheads to the glass window and watch the black box do its invisible physics, exploding our Pizza Pops from the inside out?

On the street named after a misspelled bird, there was a lot of coming and going. My parents left and returned from the hospital at all hours of the day and night. Pagers beeped and the phone rang. We went out to school and back again, and then to softball games and music lessons and to our friends' houses. The door was never locked or even closed for very long.

Our parents had been practicing medicine along parallel tracks, blazing past their lean apprenticeship years. In many ways, this was their time of shaky homeostasis, their financial high-water mark before the good times receded, but who could know it yet? My father had found a tentative peace at work. Many of his patients were farmers and hairdressers and millworkers, honest people who drank their coffee from Thermoses and ate their lunches out of brown paper bags. A few of them were immigrants themselves who brought him fruitcakes and vodka long after their stitches had come out.

This was the longest we'd lived anywhere. No matter the greener grass or farther meadows, it dawned on everyone that there might be something good, even great, about the unimaginative choice of staying put. In this pause, our material belongings piled up. The garage never housed the family cars. It became a warehouse for our parents' old-world nostalgia. In America, nearly everything was new, seemingly without history. As a kind of antidote, they bought large, afunctional pieces of heavy antique furniture that, once acquired, refused to fit through any of the household doorways. Our mother bought a five-foot-tall ornamental spinning wheel and a roll-top desk that weighed as much as a small cetacean. Our dad bought a hard couch stuffed with horsehair and a long counter from an old-time general store, another anchor to hold us down to earth. It was the eighties in all its gold-plated splendor. If a little bit was good, then more was undeniably better.

The garage was also a clearinghouse for broken objects: Christmas presents, battered toys, paired objects that had lost their soulmates. We destroyed our things almost as quickly as they came in the door. We cut them to ribbons, hungry to understand how things worked beneath the surface. We ripped the heads off dolls and bashed our Rubik's Cubes with hammers. These objects were inadequate substitutes for the things they were meant to make up for. We macerated our belongings as a form of protest, a response to something brewing in our house like a bad ferment, if only we had the words to describe it.

IN MANY WAYS, we were lucky to live with our father. He was totally unfazed by certain kid behaviors that sent North American parents into red-faced fits of apoplexy. Some things about his kids did not bother my dad—if he even noticed at all.

He was untroubled by the wastage of food, a habit of ours that disturbed our mother on a spiritual level. He was a choosy eater himself, and he seemed almost impressed by our genius when it came to the concealment of lima beans beneath plate rims, or the stowing of broccoli florets on the underside ledge of the dinner table. He paid no mind to the way we created landslides of consumer garbage, headless action figures, vivisected Cabbage Patch Kids, puppets with tangled strings, books with torn pages, bikes with bent tires.

He was untroubled by his children's incompetence when it came to tennis, hockey, lacrosse, soccer, or any other athletic activity requiring hand-eye coordination. Other parents screamed from the bleachers at their kids to perform, as if their lives depended on it. But to my dad, team sports were nothing more than extracurriculars, a diversion from the true business of life, which did not involve games.

He did not get on my case for neglecting to practice my violin. When I gave up this instrument for lack of talent, he celebrated my capitulation. It was the end of the upstairs caterwauling, of horsehair dragged across badly tuned strings, the death of my "Twinkle, Twinkle, Little Star." To him, music and the fine arts were just parlor skills. They had no serious function.

He never complained about our cupboard love, or that we used him like the Bank of Dad. It was no offense to give money to junior humans, to acknowledge the reality that children did not go to school with little briefcases or earn salaries for attending Girl Scouts. That was a Western pretense. So were children's chores, our mother's idea. These small works of capitalist theater involved shoddily performed tasks and the weekly granting of allowance—neither was worth a damn in the end. He accepted the lopsided nature of familial dependence, and its attendant fiscal hierarchies, without any doubts at all about who was at the top.

If we let our rooms descend into debris fields of biohazard detritus, he passed it by without remark. He was a messy person himself, guilty of leaving his own trails of dishware and half-consumed foodstuffs and doffed clothing throughout the house. Household entropy was not his concern or domain.

But as many habits as he was able to overlook, there were some behaviors that irked my dad down to the soles of his leather shoes. His children did crass North American things like shouting between rooms. We cursed when we thought no one was listening. We chewed with our mouths open, "just like cement mixers," according to him. We bo-

garted the technology that was meant for adults, primarily
the TV and the telephone, which were technically off-limits,
but that we used all the time behind his back. He disliked it
when we ate with our fingers foods designed for a knife and
fork. The wiping of hands, mouths, or noses on clothing.
The splatter of sauce across the kitchen lino. The spilling of
milk. The dangling of a pizza slice into one's mouth from a
small height. He did not know how to explain the vora-
ciously indiscriminate nature of our appetites, a quality our
mother compared to a locust plague descending on a field of
crops. This included the consumption of things that were
not meant for us, like his monthly fruit-basket subscrip-
tions, also gifts from his patients, that we ransacked upon
delivery before he even got home from work.

He did not like giving us rides to school or any other
place, even in the middle of blizzards. There was nowhere a
child needed to go so urgently, not compared to the adults
in the house, who had real jobs and furnished everything we
touched and ate and played with and forgot to put away.
We had legs. We could walk.

He liked a strict indoor decorum. We caught hell if we
tracked snow, mud, or mown grass beyond the front door.
We were also forbidden from monkey behavior, chasing one
another from room to room, or boisterous wrestling on the
floor. All-out brawling triggered interventions, and so did
the riding of wheeled conveyance or the playing of ball
sports anywhere but the basement—fair game, as long as he
couldn't hear us. He did not want other people's kids in his
house, which he thought of as an oasis for the grown-ups.
He couldn't abide clothing worn inside out, dirty socks, un-
brushed teeth. Any suggestion we could acquire a family pet
was enough to make his eyes bulge in disgust. He did not

want a barking terrier or a slobbering retriever shedding fur on the carpet or competing for space on his sofa. These were the rightful delineations between outside and inside, anarchy and civilization.

He expressed total aversion to our Devo, our Duran Duran. He did not want to hear "Another One Bites the Dust" on the car stereo or on the tape deck he used for playing medical audio lectures—if only we hadn't commandeered it. He did not want to hear our noise pollution on repeat or even one time through.

An irony for a doctor: He became irate when we injured ourselves by accident.

But what really stirred him to DEFCON 1 vexation was public-facing mediocrity. Cavities at the dentist. Misdemeanors at school. Whiffs of failure reflected badly on the family, and therefore him personally. What would people say? It was hard to identify who these people were, since my parents had few close friends, few guests, and no extended family anywhere in the vicinity. It didn't matter. We carried his name. He intended for us to shine, to go to the best colleges America had to offer, but alas, there was little to indicate we were headed in that direction. His barbarian spawn preferred bouncing on the neighbor's trampoline and throwing snowballs at passing cars to the obedient fulfillment of homework.

Our father didn't know much about the curriculum in our little public school. We might have been enrolled at Eton College or Princeton Day School for all he knew. He had no idea that we were learning about sexually transmitted diseases in Health Ed or square-dancing in gym class or watching Up with People shows in the school auditorium when he thought we were solving equations. Yet he always seemed to sense with telepathic accuracy the exact days when report cards were issued. No matter how discreetly we brought them into the house, no matter how we dragged our feet as we delivered them into his hands, he always knew exactly when they'd entered the premises.

He was often on the sofa, stirring his afternoon tea, usually still wearing his fancy work attire, which made these audiences even more harrowing and official. He'd study our little cards, my brother's first, and cut right past the artsy puff and the gold stars and the encouraging comments offered by Mrs. Ginder or Mrs. Thibault. He'd head right to the bottom line. We may have been twelve and in junior high, but that's where our woes began and ended.

His eye, with its surgical, laser focus, fell upon the grades at the bottom of the column, the B-minuses and the 88s. Sometimes we were sent to our rooms to contemplate the pluses and points we'd left on the table. Sometimes we received a tirade whose volume and intensity felt like a stiff gust through our hair. Sometimes both those punishments came to pass, as if we'd sinned against our ancestors, as if the dignity of the entire family had been compromised by our failure to grasp geometry or our lack of stomach for dissecting earthworms in science class.

Good grades were the rent we paid for being alive in his kingdom.

In the background, our mother was more relaxed about our academic performance. She attended our parent-teacher conferences, baked classroom cupcakes, took us to all our pageants and plays and tournaments in her reliable Toyota econobox. If we failed a test or played our squawky instruments at the back of the orchestra or if our softball mitts had holes in them, she was there to crush us with encouragement. She listened to our troubles and absorbed our tears and coached us through every wipeout. "It's all right," she'd say. "At least you tried."

Our mother's affection was easy enough. We didn't even have to try. We could bring her papier-mâché fruit bowls on Mother's Day and wizened fruit ornaments at Christmastime and receive nothing but profusions of compensatory praise. Our father's love was hard and tiny, like an uncrackable nut; it lived close to his pride and was impossible to win, therefore it cast an elusive glow. We did not truly achieve our dad's respect until later, long after we'd hammered ourselves into adult iterations, many years after it had all gone to hell.

When our mother was present for the report card readings, we'd glance up at her pleadingly for solace or escape, but she'd fold her arms and look on helplessly, as if our fate was out of her hands. *Sorry, kid. At least you tried.*

Our father had a volcanic temper, and there was little in his history or upbringing to encourage its restraint, even in the presence of weaker beings. He had moved to North America, but he was still connected, as if by tin can and string, to the ways of the old country. He was not above negative reinforcements delivered by hand or with folded reading materials—as many a child of immigrants knows—or whatever semisoft implement happened to be lying nearby. He had undoubtedly received corrections like these himself, as had his father before him, and so on for generations. And everyone turned out fine or somewhat fine, as far as anyone knew—or could know with oceans, continents, and a massive grudge in the way.

My mother's English childhood, with its tepid emotions and distant physicality, couldn't have prepared her for my dad's methods. She was accustomed to frost, whereas my dad's weapon of choice was fire. Our mother seemed to disappear in his feistier moments, fading into the wallpaper just as we wished we could.

Dad was strict, hot-blooded, and often volatile in his enactment of Indian patriarchy, but his efforts were destined for failure. His wrath came in a flash, like a thunderstorm rumbling overhead. Black clouds for one minute, sunshine the next. We knew he had a terribly short attention span and would often forget both our crimes and his punishment before the day was over.

We drove him over the edge of reason, his elder children, but he could never stop us for long. For starters, we recognized his selectivity when it came to traditional values. He often told us to "go read a book," since books were a prime modality of academic betterment, but we seldom saw him with his nose between two covers. For all his evangelizing about cognitive nutrition, he was just as susceptible as we were to the extravaganza of American TV. And unfortunately for my dad, we had inherited his unruly spirit. He was in charge, but we had plans of our own. We were young and fast. This was our natural habitat, our world, and we knew how to slip away into the underbrush.

In our after-school hours my brother and I did little homework. Instead we watched TV with glorious abandon until our father returned home. We fought over the channels, settling on *Three's Company, Gilligan's Island, Mork & Mindy,* or whatever else we could find that satisfied half our interests. But the second we heard the Corvette gurgle up in the driveway, our whole world snapped to. I'd leap into action and slap off the TV. Sometimes, if he thought of it, our dad would feel the box for signs of warmth, the clue that we'd defied his orders. Alex would slide off the sofa like a human liquid. Then we'd both dash across the carpet, crossing space virtually without touching the floor. We learned to disappear this way, with lightning stealth, so that the only person left when he entered the living room was our little sister, who could usually be found with a stack of crackers and cheese in the corner of the love seat, the only person actually reading a book.

We learned to avoid our bedrooms, because that was the first place he'd go looking for us if something was amiss. Instead, we slunk down to the basement, its dankness offset by the presence of the backup fridge where our mother stored the extra six-packs of Fresca and Tab. Or better yet, we'd slide out through the back door, dash across the dandelion farm that was our lawn, and crawl into the strip of overgrown shrubs at the back of the property, which served as a neglected fence between us and our backyard neighbors. It had a shady little hollow in the middle, a kind of no-man's-land where my father never ventured because it was a branchy tangle, unkempt and humming with mosquitoes.

But no matter the clouds gathering outside, we could only avoid the weather inside for so long.

TOWEL HEAD

FOR MY DAD, THE HOUSEHOLD RESEMBLED A PRINCELY state, a hierarchy in which benefits descended from the top of the pyramid, as with Reaganomics, trickling down to the tiny beings at the bottom. Where had this idea come from? I couldn't explain its origins, but I knew this belief was timeless and traditional, a bundle brought along from the old country, a place we knew nothing about because our father did not discuss it. Such a system might have worked on the other side of the planet, in the olden days when people wrote with quills and supped by candlelight, but I wasn't sure how it translated to 1984 in America.

Our mother conceived of the family as a little solar system held together by the force of parental gravity, a pod to be maintained with effort, sacrifice, and sometimes sheer force of will. Being Catholic, she didn't believe in divorce as a means of conflict resolution. Being Sikh, neither did our dad. Marital regret was something Americans experienced, and brazen individualism was to blame. Our mom and dad didn't believe in fighting in front of the children, either—yet more Western TMI. They waited until we were asleep or out of the house for that. Their disagreements may have transpired behind closed doors, but it didn't stop us from knowing the source of the conflict in the first place.

Our mother was overworked and under-slept, usually operating on a half dose of shut-eye each night. Sometimes we would talk to her, and it would take a long moment for her to draw her hands out of the kitchen sink foam, or to stop stirring the pot, to register she'd been spoken to, as if she'd dozed off momentarily while standing up. She leaned on outsourced domestic backup, house cleaners and baby-sitters, but with a third child, she'd blown through her last reserves and now teetered on some final threshold between organized chaos and total breakdown.

She helped us with our homework, did the laundry, scrubbed the spills, negotiated treaties for the twin battles waged during the day while she'd been out of the house saving lives. In the evenings our dad settled in on the sofa with a cup of tea, the remote control on his lap, to watch *M*A*S*H* or *All in the Family*. He didn't register her long lists of to-dos, or the many obstacles separating his wife from a pillow and horizontal darkness. In the pre-bedtime period when she was deepest in the weeds, he would do the most inadvisable thing of all—he'd tell her to stop rushing around. Whenever he uttered these words—*just relax*—my brother and I would drop whatever ruckus we were causing and spin our heads in her direction. We'd look up at her face and watch it petrify into a form of very white, fleshly stone. That was our mother. Patient, tolerant, sainted by imbalance. You could push her too far for ninety-nine days, but on the hundredth day: You better run.

She didn't get angry. She didn't threaten. She seldom raised her voice. All through my childhood, whenever I was bad, she'd cast her steely gray eyes in my direction, and whatever retributive justice she had in mind, it fell like a guillotine, swift and irreversible. If my brother and I bickered over the front seat of the car before a trip, she collected her giant purse, got out, and slammed the door with understated finality. She returned to the house, trip canceled. If we'd melted down in the grocery store, she hustled us outside to wait alone in the back seat, no matter what the thermometer said. If we lipped off when she was speaking, we could expect the total suspension of privileges with no chance of parole until she said so. Our father should have paid more attention to this parenting style. He might have learned a good lesson about what was coming.

The taxations of the workweek built to a smoldering heap of domestic dissolution: dishes in the sink, the beds unmade, the garbage cans still tipped over at the foot of the lawn. But on Fridays, despite the chaos, we often came home from school to discover our father returned early from work in a distractedly effervescent mood. We'd pause for the spectacle while he tossed clothes around in our parents' bedroom. Then he'd pack a hasty suitcase full of shiny shirts and velvet jackets and zip off in his car with scarcely a wave in our direction.

It was a two-hour drive to Montreal, a dangerous ninety minutes if the roads were snow-free. That's where he went, at least some of the time, to spend weekends without the burdens of kids or apron strings, to do just as he liked. We never really found out the full extent of these travels, at least not directly. But we investigated by sleuthing around in his pockets once his car was parked again in the driveway and his jackets had returned to their place in his bulging wardrobe. We discovered folded scraps of hotel stationery, partially smoked Du Maurier cigarette packages, matchbooks from restaurants, much of it written in French.

What else did he get up to, and did our mother know? She returned home on Friday nights later than everyone else. She walked in through the door, often with grocery bags dangling from her wrists, then set down her burdens at the threshold, including her keys and tremendous hobo handbag, which she released with a relieved thud. She cast her eye upon the scene like a weary disaster-management specialist. Her assessment of the home front took in all its persons, missing and present, at which point she decided to make the best of our imperfect situation.

In the winter, our mother took us cross-country skiing on Saturdays or tobogganing on Sundays. In the warmer months she planned field trips that capitalized on our dad's absence, since he never enjoyed any of our family hobbies if they happened to take place in nature. She packed her car with sleeping bags, a big orange cooler, and a heavy canvas tent among many other items, bulky and sundry, a load that left scarcely enough room for the children to fit. My mother loved camping and canoeing; she'd grown up in the city, but in North America she became an outdoor enthusiast, an autodidact in the wilderness arts of foraging and fire-building. It was the thing we did when my dad was not around or when we needed a break from his company, since his idea of camping was the Four Seasons Hotel with twenty-four-hour room service. It was one thing we could do and know he'd never come along.

At the same time, we didn't understand why he needed vacations from us, and this was confusingly painful, since his extracurricular sojourns also provided us with the collateral benefits of a dad-free household. Many years later he'd confess to me, in his haphazard, accidental way, some of the mystery destinations he'd visited on the weekends without us. Montreal, Chicago. Once, he flew to Europe on the Concorde jet, a freebie from a businessman friend he'd picked up along the way, someone we never met.

We also failed to understand why our mother did little to foil these wanderings. She was a peacemaker at heart, at least that's how it looked. But that's not what she was really up to. She was collecting receipts, adding them up, filing them away for future reference.

WHEN I WAS THIRTEEN, I saw *Indiana Jones and the Temple of Doom* for the first time. In one scene, the swashbuckling Harrison Ford is invited to a lavish dinner by the boy-maharaja of Pankot, with many turbaned, bearded guests in attendance. They're served eyeball soup and chilled monkey brains while women in lehengas gyrate with castanets in the background. Later on in the story, a man's heart is torn out by an evil Hindu priest, and then he's lowered into a sacrificial fire—quite a bit of gore for a culture partial to vegetarianism.

In the *Temple of Doom* days, there were still hardly any actual Indian characters on TV or at the movies, just like there were few deadbeat dads or single moms shedding tears into their Friday-night merlot. There were few divorces until *Kramer vs. Kramer,* and even then, many parents wouldn't let their kids watch it, as if the film captured something all too real for depiction, something never narrated in public, let alone shared in a cinema with strangers. I learned that shame lived in the silence.

We saw *Gandhi,* starring Ben Kingsley in a dhoti, but who really knew what Ben Kingsley was in his shapeshifting demi-darkness—Indian? English? A bit of both? When people thought of on-screen Indians, they still remembered Peter Sellers in brownface. In *The Party,* Sellers plays Hrundi V. Bakshi, a bungling Indian actor with a dippy, faux-subcontinental accent who shows up at a tasteful Hollywood soirée wearing a tan suit, an orange tie, and matching orange socks with white shoes. Bakshi is cursed with a bumbling curiosity, utterly unaware of his own silliness. The guests are amused by this runty brown fellow—until Bakshi stumbles through a series of inadvertent gaffes and utterly destroys the event. Hilarious, wasn't it, the way Indianness fit so well with slapstick?

In the thick of *The Party*'s disaster, the host demands, "Who do you think you are?"

Bakshi replies with surprising backbone, "In India, we don't think who we are, we know who we are."

The shambling middle-aged man with a penchant for loud wardrobe choices, with a paralyzed sense of social awareness and a total exemption from Marlboro Man masculinity. The joke was obviously on my dad. But a defiant form of dignity belied Bakshi's oblivion. A human paradox. A layered consciousness. This also felt familiar.

On the other hand, I learned a lot about ideal American life from TV, from shows like *Family Ties,* which featured a monochromatic household with three normal kids and two normal parents. The dad, Steven Keaton, was an ex-hippie public radio station manager whose humbly carefree attitude about his own appearance expressed itself in rumpled plaid shirts, a beard, and shaggy hair. Steven Keaton did not dress like a peacock or wear scent bombs of cologne, and when he drank tea, he did not require royalty-grade tray service complete with a miniature milk pitcher and sugar bowl. Father Keaton made hot beverages for himself using just a regular tea bag and a plain mug and water poured directly from the kettle. He appeared, despite the light sit-com conflicts, to be unswervingly devoted to his wife and best friend, Elyse. In one episode, he's faced with a sexy blond co-worker who throws herself at his feet. He may have been tempted, but he possessed enough foresight to realize an affair would obliterate his world from the inside out. He knew there were no true secret compartments in life, no matter how much he might wish for them. Everything— his private self, his work, his family—was connected to everything else.

I gleaned a lot at my friends' houses, too. Their dads called their kids "sweetheart" and "buddy." They commu-nicated with their offspring about the minutiae of life just as easily as they played catch with Nerf footballs out on their diagonally mowed lawns. They knew what time school started and who had last walked the dog. They could not be snowed by their kids because they knew every contour and wrinkle of their days. And despite the odd bout of gaslight-ing applied to their daughters' emotions, or homophobic hazing used as discipline for their sons, they were mostly kind and devoted, or at least that's the way they looked to me.

They did the sacrificial grunt work of the patriarchy. They blacktopped their driveways and repaired their own cars and emptied and refilled their aboveground swimming pools every year just so we could cannonball off the decks in the heated days of summer vacation. They ate the bread heels and the charred hot dogs. They drove their daughters to early-morning swim practice, and they sometimes picked me up on the way. They often took me along on their family adventures, my American proxy dads, and in their company, I figured out how to water-ski, how to feed a woodstove, how to sharpen a knife. Sometimes these were overt lessons, but mostly I learned by osmosis.

American fathers conspired with their children against mom directives; they let us eat Pringles before dinner and play hours of *Adventure* on the rec room Atari. They talked with their kids using a different language than the one mothers used, a kind of semi-violent joshing in which they played the older siblings.

"Don't worry," they said, holding pillows to their kids' faces. "This might only hurt a little bit."

They sprayed their children with garden hoses and flogged them with the towels left wet on the bathroom floor. They could call their kids smelly or lazy or useless idiots, without meaning it in the slightest; these were terms of endearment. They let their kids razz them, too, and no one's pride was harmed. North American families looked to me like soft republics in which everyone, even the small people, if they didn't exactly get a vote, at least they got a lobby. In the dream, everyone's needs were considered.

WE KNEW, MY twin and I, that our parents were unconventional, even when we thought of them separately. Together, they were totally unlike any other parents we'd ever met or read about or seen march across a silver screen. By logical extension this meant we were weirdos as well, a fate worth escaping, if only it were possible.

Our dad was one-of-a-kind. He was extra. As a form of relief, my twin and I built a blackly comedic fiction about the activities our father got up to when he left the house without us. These stories took place in smoky underground bars. They featured nocturnal lizard-men with swollen eyes and cigarettes burning down between their fingers. Or women with frosted blond hair straight from our mental database of made-for-TV movies: *Death of a Centerfold, Calendar Girl Murders,* and *Secret Weapons,* starring Linda Hamilton and Geena Davis as Russian honeypot spies. My brother was a talented cartoonist, and he illustrated with the colored pens and markers that our mother had bought for us, probably imagining the trees, rainbows, and ponies we'd be drawing instead. We also crafted a farcical narrative about an imaginary alternative dad, a nameless white dude in Birkenstocks, a fishing vest, and a swagman's cork hat, the guy our mother might have married had she not been hooked by our dad back in the sixties. We knew our mother well. As it turns out, our guy was not too far from the man she'd marry many years later, the second time around.

Every time my dad descended the stairs in a silk shirt and gold chain, with an un-American number of buttons undone, his hair combed back, in the costume of his hidden life, our eyes would fall on these details, and we'd share a jaded sneer. We'd track him out the door as he left without so much as a goodbye. We'd listen for the gunning of his engine, the scrape of the undercarriage as he reversed over the lump at the end of the driveway. Then our race to the TV began, followed by a battle royale for the remote control. Our fights were never just fights. At heart they were a war for the scarcest resources in the house.

The story of our dad's alternate life survived even though we knew no actual bathrobed floozies, nor sleazy associates. We'd never met anyone like that. Our dad was a village physician, specializing in everything and nothing. He attended to townsfolk with urological problems. But satire is an underling art form, the comedy of the powerless. It gave us the illusion of agency, a way of reclaiming something that our dad couldn't touch or probably even understand. We were happy when he was gone from the house, our freedom regained, but it felt complicated. We regretted the father we had, but also missed the one who'd left, and beyond that, the one who might have existed, if my father had been a different person, from a different country, born in another era. We loved our dad, but we didn't like him. We feared him. But a more pointed reality had begun to sink in: He did not like us much, either.

We knew he was Indian and that he'd grown up in East Africa—places that existed in the shadowy lands of our imagination just like our invented subterranean worlds. He came from an archaic tradition whose customs misaligned with the world as we knew it. But he was also a misfit when it came to these original values. He'd chosen our mother, for a start. He'd also come from a culture in which family and fatherhood were everything, but he wasn't really made for its togetherness—not as a matter of preference, but on what felt like a fundamental, almost cellular level.

And although he was fearsome and annoying to live with, I also felt a little bit bad for him. If I asked him for money to buy a pair of back-to-school jeans, he'd give me five dollars or one hundred dollars with no appropriate amount in between. He didn't know how much kids' clothing cost or even where on earth our mother took us to procure such things. He knew how to stop an arterial bleed, but he seemed clueless about the standard operating procedures of basic living. He was forgetful and inconsistent. He'd been prepared for a different adulthood, a wholly separate life that didn't exist in the world he'd built for himself, at least not anymore.

When he went to parties and gatherings, our dad sometimes hovered at the outer edges as if pushed there by social currents, looking wounded about not being at the center. He did not really know when people were just being polite. He did not always get the joke. He seemed impervious to the emotional layers, the subtext, the unspoken strata of intention. He was too busy trying to swim along on the surface.

IN AMERICA, THE eighties were a time of orthodontic innovations, a phase of widespread teenage headgear and glinting metal smiles. By thirteen, I had a crowded set of adult teeth and my own unfortunate mouthful of silvery hardware. My braces were tightened on the regular, and after visits to the dental office, my face hurt at the slightest touch, even from contact with a pillow. This ache aligned with a growth spurt that racked my shins at night, as if my body was in a tussle with itself, as if it didn't know which way it wanted to grow. My hair had decided to push out half-wavy, half-straight. The skin darkened on my forehead but lightened in white patches on my cheeks.

In my family, we seldom talked about race. Our house was a refuge, the place where we could be ourselves, a unit, without differences and unevenness. We could try, at least, even if it seemed impossible. My brother and I rarely discussed our ethnic composition, either. For starters, it seemed obvious to us. Half-English, half-Indian. No confusion there. But at school, and out in the world, we faced the same unspoken quandaries. Home was a reprieve from the duplicities of playing both sides.

Biracial. I knew what this word meant, at least in theory, but not as a concept that applied to me. I seldom heard it spoken aloud, not when I ventured over to my friends' houses and not at school and not in the grocery store or our village's tiny public library. Not on the nightly news. Not on any after-school special. I lived semi-gratefully in the gap, if not purely Caucasian, then sufficiently off-white to be lumped in with my peers in the majority. I didn't protest or correct. At thirteen, few things made me happier than blending into a crowd. But I had a squidgy, nameless feeling, a hunch that I was getting away with something, a kind of hiding out.

Those days, in the immoderate thick of the eighties, I heard ethnic jokes and racial nicknames fall out of the mouths of the kids in my classes. They uttered these phrases accidentally and on purpose, occasionally just beyond earshot, often when I was standing right there beside them. Sometimes they repeated things their parents had said, or perhaps it was self-inspiration. These names applied to theoretical Black and brown people who lived in faraway places, never right here at home. I heard "towelhead" for the first time, a word tossed around in reference to people of Arabic or Muslim descent. But who really knew anyone of that extraction? Who among us had any distinctions? "Towelhead," as I understood its usage, was shorthand for anyone who looked vaguely brown and wore a textile headdress. But who would have known a Paki or a towelhead if one walked right up and shook their hand? Or tended their torn ACLs in the emergency room, or tweezed the broken glass from their foreheads whenever they crashed their cars?

Once upon a time, when I went out in public with my dad, he'd held my hand whenever we crossed the street. But I was too old for that now. In fact, I'd stopped walking next to him altogether. I preferred to sulk along behind in the wake of his cologne, studying his suit jacket vents, single or double depending on the day, as if to pretend we were strangers—a behavioral quirk he liked to blame on teenage hormones. I didn't like walking next to him, for starters, because he was always telling me to stand up straight or to rearrange my facial expression so I didn't look like I'd been eating lemons. But I had other reasons, too.

It was so much easier to walk next to my mother. I'd taken her side before I really knew my reasons why, before I understood that there could be sides in the first place when, in theory, at least, we were all on the same team. I didn't know the consequences of this decision I'd made without even realizing it, that it would be the hairline crack that grew and divided me from my dad. This space would widen as time passed into a broad valley where all kinds of life would transpire without him.

But at the time, it didn't really seem like a choice between white and brown so much as a preference for Mom over Dad. I knew he was difficult, eccentric, and chronically inconvenient in part because he'd been built from foreign components. But some portion of his basic nature was to blame for this difference also. I couldn't tell the ratio, couldn't identify where the line existed between personality and culture, and I'm not sure he could, either. The whole thing became a mess, with all the bits melded, so it was hard, if not impossible, to pull the ingredients apart. It wasn't simply a question of skin, or belonging, or the Englishness of Mom, or the Indianness of Dad, or some murky middle state in between. It had become a curry of emotion and allegiance and identity, everything cooked together, all at once.

HOW SHOULD A DAUGHTER BE?

ND THEN, INEVITABLY, CAME THE DAYS OF *SIXTEEN Candles,* my Noxzema years, a time of studied teenage self-formulation. The beginning of the end of innocence.

My idea of acceptable female personhood was heavily researched, often within the pages of *Sweet Valley High,* a novel series whose main characters were twins named Jessica and Elizabeth Wakefield. Their father was a lawyer, and their mother was an interior designer—a perfectly successful vanilla family. But most importantly, Jessica and Elizabeth were beautiful, blond California girls, forever sixteen and the perfect size six.

I also learned a lot about the elusory nature of ideal femininity from my subscription to *Seventeen* magazine, which sandwiched dating advice columns between ads for Gunne Sax prairie dresses and high-collared shirts with not a clavicle or an inch of décolletage in sight. Cautionary articles about herpes and AIDS ran opposite photos of wedding china and engagement rings, and recipes for skim-milk breakfast smoothies sat next to the girl-athlete heroines of the 1984 Olympics who'd turned to shilling for fast-food companies. They could get away with eating Big Mac calorie bombs, this juxtaposition implied, because they were not like the rest of us. They were superhuman.

The summer before high school, my friends and I spent a good part of our vacation marinating in baby oil, roasting on backyard decks or at the town beach. Every day, someone went home looking like a hot dog pulled from boiling water, but it was never me. I just got more tanned no matter what I did, without a squirt of sunblock applied to a square inch of my body. Still, it took me quite a while to realize that I wasn't a white girl, at least not all the way through—a painfully slow epiphany that wouldn't resolve for quite some time, if it ever did at all.

These were the days of Sun-In, a peroxide product in a spray bottle, perfumed to smell like the beach. We spritzed our hair, or soaked it to dripping, before heading anywhere outside. My friends came away with gorgeous lemon-colored streaks, but nothing good happened to me. At best, all I got was a brassy overtone that made me feel like a Russ Berrie troll doll. My hair wasn't sleek or effortlessly wavy, either, not like the coifs of my dreams. Mine was a halo of frizz that refused to lie down in silky submission no matter the sprays or gels or heat I applied. I resented my hair for its unbleachable darkness, the way it cowlicked yet still wouldn't hold a curl. It was my dad's hair—just stubbornly itself.

Hair. The older I got, the more Indian it became. It

wouldn't abide, and yet now there were worrying profusions of it, sprouting from everywhere. My mother, with her poreless skin and invisible body hair, couldn't truly understand my plight. But I had Nair on my side. I smeared its brimstone-scented emulsion on my legs, armpits, and bikini zone, a phrase that implied a tiny, demure patch of the body, not an area that spread alarmingly onto one's thighs. I waited through the tingly burn while the hairs melted inside their follicles, then I washed those black squiggles down the drain.

The performance of femininity was quite possibly the last thing on my mother's mind. She had two teens, a second grader, and my dad to contend with—bigger trees to fell, if not an entire forest. She didn't color her hair, which had turned a silvery nut brown. She favored practical fashion, big skirts with big pockets and no-iron trousers in a time when most of the village moms wore big hair, shoulder pads, and jewelry that could signal satellites. She wore snow boots in winter and sensible sandals in summer. She didn't wear heels or much makeup at all beyond the odd dash of shimmery eyeshadow when it was time to get dressed for a dinner out, which happened less and less those days. Nobody really wanted to hang out together anymore. My father mostly ventured out on the town without us.

My dad, despite being a dandy himself, disapproved of adornment when it came to his daughters. Any detour from modesty was verboten—no shiny things to catch the eye, no divergence at all from the unadulterated state of girlhood. He totally forbade me from the use of cosmetics, which was a piercing heartbreak as far as I was concerned, since it meant missing out on the bounty of modern cosmetic extravagances: cherry-red lip glosses, mood lipsticks, electric-blue mascaras.

For a man who knew nothing about which Shakespeare play I was reading in English class or what leg of the medley relay I swam during meets, he noticed every little modification I made to my appearance. He hit the ceiling when I got my ears pierced—just once in each lobe with tiny gold studs. I'm pretty sure my dad would have preferred it if I wore a pinafore complete with ankle socks and double-folded braids tied with ribbons, a quintessential look for Indian schoolgirls. He wouldn't have minded if I remained suspended in childhood until I moved out from beneath his guardianship into whatever semi-autonomous state he had in mind for me postgraduation.

Whenever I tried to get away with a pinky nail of glitter polish, or a microscopic iota of accessorized fun, he sensed it almost omnisciently, almost before the lipstick had been unsheathed or the perfume atomized. Nevertheless, his rules were my induction into the world of beauty subterfuge. Eventually, I'd amass a clandestine collection of frosty pink blush and purple eyeliner pencils. I'd deploy them with a skill mastered in the back seats of my friends' getaway cars with scarcely the use of a mirror. But in the meantime, he could smell my hairspray while I was still walking up the driveway and detect the thinnest sheen of Bonne Bell on my lips from the other side of the room.

I was afflicted with acne, and this really seemed to snag my dad's attention. I would sometimes catch his physician's eye as it roved around my face, connecting the angry dots. He suggested my inflammatory problems might be addressed with microdermabrasion in a dermatologist's office, even though no specialists like this practiced anywhere close by. I didn't like my skin, either, and spent plenty of time attacking it with Ten-O-Six and Buf-Pufs. But the thought of traveling long distances to have my pimples sandblasted felt terribly depressing, as if such a radical treatment was an acknowledgment of my facial hideousness. My mother nixed this idea. My skin woes weren't a deathly pox. They were a normal part of growing up.

Increasingly, my dad mistrusted my hours of free time. He didn't really like me to leave the house except for sanctioned activities like school and sports practice. If I asked to go to a movie, he'd phone around to random parent-friends to discover if the film was age-appropriate. Was there violence or nudity? Was it suitable for a girl? He had no idea, no inkling at all, that the movie was just my cover story for staying out past curfew. He never realized that I attended school dances where boys and girls shuffled awkwardly to Air Supply and Styx while stiffly embraced, their hands sliding southward until the chaperones slapped them back up again. Sometimes my comrades brought along secret stashes of crème de menthe or root beer schnapps skimmed from their parents' liquor cabinets—a scandal that would have reduced my dad to ashes.

He did not like any of my friends. These girls were white and American and therefore prone to Western excesses like academic underperformance and teen pregnancy. But he also resented our female closeness, the way we compared notes and discussed everything to death in melodramatic and excruciating detail in the kitchen, where our family phone, a wall-mounted antique replica with a very short cord, occupied the Times Square of the household. "Always in each others' pockets," he'd mutter, shaking his head.

Boyfriends and dating: so verboten they existed in the unmentionable shadows. My mother, being Catholic, also leaned on tradition, at least when it came to the parenting of teenagers. She disapproved of hellion activities like premarital sex, drinking, and smoking weed, and often enough her values coincided with my dad's restrictions. But her case was compromised, too, because by then my brother and I had begun to doubt the deliberate, well-planned story of our familial origins. We saw perfectly well the way our parents tumbled headlong into major life decisions, into love, with scarcely a deliberation or a backward glance.

Fortunately for my dad, he had the cruelties of adolescence on his side. By the time I hit freshman year I'd shot up past my brother in height. I stuck out in a crowd of schoolmates like a giraffe grazing shrubs on the savanna. I wore high-water hems and was hopelessly flat-chested, a bodily feature I tried to conceal with baggy sweaters and textbooks clutched tight. But there was no disguising anything anymore. It was open season on pubescent girlhood. No womanly bump or curve failed to escape the notice of the big-mouthed boys who patrolled our high school hallways, as if that was now their purpose, to observe their classmates' development, to snap bra straps, and when no teachers were looking, to shove the girls up against the lockers to cop feels. It felt strange to be treated like a sheltered know-nothing at home, and yet to run this daily gauntlet. Everywhere my friends and I went, males gave color commentary about our bodies, as if we didn't know how we looked, as if they were doing us a favor. We were a form of unclaimed public property, available for everyone's gaze, even grown men in the street.

But my dad didn't see any of that. He still thought of my

school as an idyllic place of quiet study and diligent peda-
gogical striving. He thought he could protect me just by saving me from myself.

MY FATHER'S ENIGMAS unfolded in ever-surprising ways. In
some respects, he seemed not to care at all about gender
distinctions. He rejected the staid habits of North American
maleness, opting instead for more flamboyant means of self-
expression. My dad was perfectly secure in his heterosexual-
ity. He possessed the surety of an Indian man, whose
masculinity needed no reinforcement because it was never in
doubt in the first place, backed as it was by centuries of un-
defeated solidity. He didn't need a big truck with a lift kit or
a man cave full of power tools. He chose hot pink over navy
blue. When deep in conversation, he thought nothing of
touching other men on the shoulder or forearm. He felt no
need, as other men did, to stand far apart talking in moder-
ate shouts.

Occasionally, if we ventured into a store together, my
dad would run his fingers over a silky scarf or a piece of
jewelry that caught his eye.

"But that's for women," I'd say.

He'd just shrug and try it on.

But he also saw the world as a pigeonholed place, its
people divided from one another by the material circumstances of their lives. He'd fallen victim to inequality himself, so it confused me that he could believe in such deep
partitions—male versus female—a split in his worldview
dividing one half of the world's population from the other.
For my dad, gender was a timeless and immutable thing, like
a canyon carved out by the flow of an ancient river. Gender

was a tautology. There need not be any empirical evidence to support it. It just *was,* like weather, or the fact of gravity.

I could tell he thought of females as a nurturing clean-up crew whose primary job it was to fulfill the needs of the household and everyone in it, but especially to attend to the men. I saw this in the way he talked to women out in public, the servers and flight attendants, with a casual certainty that they would drop whatever they were doing, no matter how pressing, and carry out his wishes. He talked to them without greetings or preliminaries, as if they had no need at all for introductions.

He didn't mind the company of women. Indeed, he loved having us around, ambiently puttering in the next room or listening at his elbow. But his favorite kind of human togetherness was parties and social gatherings at which the men hived off from the women in the classic living room–kitchen divide. He would gravitate immediately to the guy side of the equation, where he believed the true intellectual capital was found.

He accepted, and sometimes repeated, the Western joke that women were twee, appearance-obsessed airheads who'd do anything for a hailstone-sized diamond and a rich spouse, or that they liked to shop and spend money on pointless, gaudy things. I chalked this up to subconscious projection because in our house there was only one person with flashy tastes and wanton spending habits, and it wasn't our mother. She was a workaholic who dressed like a missionary and drove a Dodge Colt, her next no-frills car after the Tercel.

At home, all the domestic drudgery seemed to slide downhill in my mother's direction, even though she worked longer hours than he did and was his economic equal—maybe even his better. And increasingly, as I transitioned from child to woman, the management of dust and dirt fell to me as well.

If there was laundry to be ported from one floor to the next, or the return of objects to their rightful place, or any process involving soap and water, I often found myself at the end of my father's pointer finger. I chafed beneath these as-signments, but not because of the work itself. In our family experiment, I had a control group, my twin brother, who was precisely my age yet exempt from most of the above. Somehow he got to wear his shaggy hair and disintegrating tube socks and go out with his friends almost whenever he pleased. He slunk around with few comments from our dad about his appearance or comportment. The hot beam of my dad's attention burned him in other ways. There was no report-card grade that was good enough, no test result that could pass muster. My brother faded beneath this constant pressure. I could see it in the way he slunk and slouched and crept around the house on tiptoe in an effort to avoid notice. He mumbled when he talked, a language that nobody could understand except our mother and sometimes me, if I was close enough to hear it. It was as if my brother was in train-ing for some kind of scholastic death match that only my dad could foresee. I had to deliver excellent grades, too, but when my dad wanted a cup of tea or a snack fixed or a spill to be mopped from the floor, it was never my brother's homework that got interrupted.

These were the paradox years, my time of prominence and invisibility. My dad became hypervigilant about my ap-pearance and whereabouts. But at the same time, I began to dematerialize in his presence, vanishing a little more each month. At fourteen, I was practically see-through. If we kept going at this rate, soon I'd be antimatter. To reclaim a little of my own substance, I worked hard to hit the honor roll every semester, to avoid his wrath but also to make him happy. But my gold stars had lost their luster. Predictability was dull. And nobody liked a try-hard.

It seemed my dad wanted daughters who were beautiful but invisible, slim but not athletic, educated but not too smart. He pushed a version of femaleness that was impossibly conflicted—almost appealing in its lofty contradictions. I was encouraged to perform at the highest academic level so I could one day attend a superior school and become a first-class working professional. But at the same time, I should get used to the role of subordinate and helper. How were those two trajectories, the servant with the A-type, meant to square?

It twisted my brain to contemplate these contradictions, but he refused to explain them to me. It flustered him that I even asked. How could he reject his traditional values on the one hand while demanding them back at the same time? In the end, I'm not sure even he could square his old-man Indian side with his modern expectations, as if the paradox led him to a strange, ruminative place.

My dad wanted me to integrate, but only when it came to the grindstone parts of American life. All the questionable stuff, the sugar, the caffeine, the R-rated movies, the after-dark hijinks, the boys, the sparkle, the jumping from great heights, all of that was off-limits, even though I could see perfectly well that he indulged in the unfettered delights of Western living himself—the junk food, the TV, his weekends away, his unexplained late nights out—leaving our long-suffering mother to pick up the slack. Adulthood confused me with its brazen hypocrisies. It didn't seem fair at all.

My irritation was topical at first, but the further I

marched into young womanhood, the hotter those sentiments became. It wasn't just the loss of my free-range childhood privileges, it was the principle behind these new
constraints, the unevenness of their distribution, and the
underlying worldview. That's what really chapped my mood.
But whenever I piped up, my dad squelched my complaints
by blaming them, as he often did, on the haywire chemistry
of a young woman's brain. I didn't know what to call this
rhetorical technique, not yet, but it burned me to think that
teenagers, girls especially, were only capable of single-ply
emotions, divested of any agency or reason. My opinions
had substance, I felt sure, a basis in reality just like anyone
else's. And as far as I could tell, my dad was the only high-
tempered person in the house, the only one capable of totally losing it if the wind blew his feathers in the wrong
direction.

So that's what I did. I blew in the wrong direction. Why
did I have to accept the rules without any explanation of
their logic? Why was it okay for adults to do the very things
they'd banned their children from even contemplating? Why
did my brother have it so good?

Why?

Why?

Why?

Whenever I dared to persist in my objections, I could almost see the little blood vessels swelling in the whites of my
dad's eyes. Backtalk was disobedience on a scale beyond
comprehension, and whenever I sprinkled it around, my dad
could pass from serene to supernova in under a minute.

He expected me to receive his temper without fighting
back, even though this was an inherited impossibility. We'd
been stamped from the same machine, and I'd received his

snappy attitude as a matter of cellular reproduction. But I backed down from these showdowns, knowing that if I pushed it too far there was a good chance I'd never leave the house or see daylight again, at least until he forgot all about my rebellion and moved on to the next thing. I'd save it for another day, some unformed time in the future when I'd grown the courage to fight it out to the bitter end.

My brother knew better than to get involved. He waged his own battles with our father.

And no matter what she believed, our mother was a peace-loving person who shied from conflict. When it came to my dad, she advised me a thousand times to tone it down.

"Catch more flies with honey," she said.

"But why should I have to catch flies at all?" I argued.

If my grandmother had been in my life, she might have tossed her head back and laughed out loud at my plight. She might have told me that I had it *good*. I was lucky to have this nirvana of academic possibilities just waiting around my next corner. All this inconvenience that was cramping my style? Ha! This was just the warm-up for a marathon, my first taste of a system that was older and more everlasting than one birdbrained teenager could ever imagine. It wasn't about to vanish just because I snapped my fingers. The apparatus derived from the old ways of the old country, where a young woman's chastity, modesty, and compliant demeanor determined her marriageability, her future, her everything. Heavy were her burdens, since she was the guardian of the family honor, carried as it was by women and girls, not in their minds but in the vessels of their bodies.

And exactly who invented this way of living? I'd ask in reply. Whoever it was, they probably never considered how this chauvinistic brainwashing might float in a brand-new world. I'd already watched *9 to 5,* in which Lily Tomlin, Jane Fonda, and Dolly Parton, the holy trinity of movie feminism, spiked their evil boss's coffee with rat poison. We weren't in the village anymore, were we? We were in North America, where a girl could eat Smurf-Berry Crunch while flipping pages of *The Clan of the Cave Bear* or *The Valley of Horses* right there at the kitchen table. These books featured a badass blond Cro-Magnon protagonist, Ayla, who hunts with a slingshot and has sex with her preternaturally well-endowed boyfriend, Jondalar, whose duty it was, pre-Ayla, to deflower virgins. Never mind that, even to me, a teenage girl's virginal chalice seemed like a terrible place to stow anything for safekeeping, let alone the reputation of the whole family line.

If I'd had brown-eyed desi girls for friends, I'd have realized it was normal to have at least one weird, fixated parent who circled over you like a chicken hawk no matter what you did, good or bad, even if you lived like a Buddhist nun. It wasn't a punishment; these were just the prevailing conditions of an Indian daughter's life. I'd have learned that it was typical that different rules applied to sons and daughters. Inequality wasn't personal, it was just tradition, a neutral force to be outlived and outsmarted. I could also expect to be unfavorably compared to most of my cousins for the rest of my life, or any other immigrant kid in town who happened to hit the valedictorian bell, no matter how terminally eggheaded or socially impaired they were. I'd have known that piercings, tattoos, or any kind of body adornment were inadvisable, as if the entire canvas of our femininity had to remain unmarked, despite the fact that our very own grandmothers owned enough inherited bling to light up the Rockefeller Center Christmas tree—nose rings and toe rings, anklets and bangles, solid gold finery so whopping it could be measured by the pound. If I'd had South Asian girlfriends, I'd have known that paradox was all part of the deal, and even though it made no sense at all, it was not for us to question.

But I didn't have brown girlfriends or grandparents whose wisdom I might fall back on. I had my mother, who'd been schooled by nuns, and my dad, in whose pockets the old-country ways had been smuggled, even if he didn't always know it. They were doing their very level best, fumbling through, trying to make sense of this newfangled place with its never-ending parade of mystifications, such as adults rioting over Cabbage Patch dolls or Boy George in full glam. Was it any wonder they retreated to what was safe and known? Who could blame them for backing down from the pioneer movements of their younger days, the avant-garde that had brought them together in the first place?

They tried to shepherd their flock successfully through to adulthood. On the journey, they expected us to embrace all the studious, hardworking aspects of life, while sitting on the sidelines for all the good stuff—the loud, open-air festival of American youth. In response, we bleated hard, the same question over and over: If you didn't want us to live in this world, then why did you bring us here?

A MOONBEAM FROM LIGHTNING

I N 1986, CHERNOBYL MELTED DOWN. THIS WAS A SHAD-
owy incident at the edge of Ukraine, then on the far side
of the Iron Curtain. Chernobyl featured no world-ending
detonation, no mushroom cloud, not as our school-aged
atomic dreams had once portended. Its main event was tiny,
a deceptively small steam explosion inside a nuclear reactor
unit. But this crisis of overpressure triggered a full-on collapse, which then spewed invisible radioactive fallout far
and wide. All the residents were evacuated from the sur-
rounding area, and they never went back to a region that
would eventually be called, in the poetry of cataclysm, the
Zone of Alienation. It amazed me how one small rupture
could cause so much long-term devastation.

In the summer, just before high school resumed, I went
back to swim practice, lugging my duffel bag and towels.

One of my teammates stopped me in the locker room. "I'm sorry your parents split up," she said.

"Oh," I joked. "Did they?"

It was sophomore year, or maybe I was a junior. Or perhaps the breakup spread over all those semesters—a blur, a numbness, a trudge-march through a blizzard of happenings, all surprising yet inevitable.

Some families drift apart slowly. Some bust up suddenly, with a single reverberating crack. Others get nibbled away at the edges or consumed from the inside out until just a shell is left. Maybe it's money. Or irreconcilable differences. Or conflicted parenting styles. Or infidelity. Maybe it's all of the above. My parents' reasons were not particularly special, except in one respect. Their marriage had been built from the stuff of collided worlds, moonbeams and lightning. Their split wasn't just personal. It was a failure of cross-cultural understanding. And if they couldn't keep it together, two people who'd slept side by side for nearly two decades, who'd laughed at each other's jokes, who'd cared for each other at some point and perhaps still did, then what hope was there for the rest of the world, for factions and nations who loathed each other from a distance? What hope was there for *all you need is love* when love was just the bare minimum, necessary but not sufficient?

My father had spent years living in his own little world, despite my mother's objections. Nothing she did or said seemed to have any lasting effect on his habits. He was simply who he was, so incontrovertibly himself it was practically commendable. He'd tested her stamina, through all the parenting burdens she'd carried alone, the school concerts and sporting events and parent-teacher meetings and pediatricians' appointments. Through all the nights she'd made dinner after a long day at the hospital, all the times he'd sniffed and rejected those aromas, sauntering out into the night alone in search of better fare. All the Fridays he'd stymied her family weekend plans then vaporized in his fast cars to parts unknown, or to places revealed once the credit card statements whispered in through the mail. Through all the bills she'd paid with her own wages, the cash she'd hidden from him in the tampon boxes beneath her bathroom sink. Through the hundreds of his shirts that she'd washed, all the telltale objects she'd discovered in his pockets, the matchboxes, the rumpled cocktail napkins, the telephone numbers scratched on little rips of paper. The many times we'd lobbied like a couple of junior aides, a twin on each side, pleading with her to do something finally, even though we had no idea what *something* meant—realistically, economically, even spiritually—what it might cost from her point of view.

He'd ground her down over the years, our brave, persevering, tragically tolerant mother, until finally she was reduced to an elemental, pulverized form, at which point an alchemical transformation took place. She began to reconstitute, to assemble again into a different shape, one built from the filaments of an icy substance we recognized from her rare disciplinary moments. This metamorphosis happened slowly at first, but then it built with a swiftness and fierce exactitude the likes of which we'd never seen before. One day, our calm, pacifist parent blew her stack. Our mother, who was maxed out all the time, who never got a sleep-in unless she'd slipped a disc, who had scarcely a moment alone to drink a glass of water in its entirety—finally, she reached the end of her long, frayed rope.

Finito, as she liked to say.

. . .

HOW DOES AN epiphany occur? In our world, not as a thunderclap, but like an avalanche waiting to let go.

One day our mother decided to move in closer, to finally get down and dirty with the particulars she'd been too overwhelmed to truly examine, the ones she'd always sensed were there. During her investigations, she found out that her nemesis had a name, but it wasn't Candace or Linda or Stephanie. In the end it was American Express, the little green plastic card with its trusty helmeted centurion, which in her case was like an express ticket to somewhere interesting, all right. Our father never left home without it.

One day my mother's eye fell upon a credit card statement whose left-hand column of entries contained a puzzle of unknown names, places, and things. And on the right-hand side, a dizzying cascade of digits and zeros all the way down to a vertigo-inducing number at the bottom line. She pulled at this thread, and before long the rest unraveled. The initial discovery sent her down a forensic accounting wormhole, and if her stomach had dropped at the first sight of dollar signs it continued to free-fall with each page. Billing cycle by billing cycle, each statement she peeled back revealed new layers of intrigue. She added it all up forward and backward and found that our father had spent an eye-popping amount of money, had blown his way through their hard-earned reserves and then some. And then to really frost the cake, he'd enthusiastically splurged some more.

An awareness that had once been amorphous now became concrete. All the tumblers aligned and clicked into place. Our spontaneous, fun-loving, adventure-seeking father, who lacked any sense of fiscal restraint or limit, would keep going unchecked until he drove the family wagon over the cliff—he was well on the way to that end—unless she did something about it. And finally, once she registered this hazardous teetering on the compromised edge, it was no longer a question of marital inconvenience or personal forbearance or asking what Jesus would do. She hadn't yet reached the bottom of the stack, but that's when she stopped counting.

After that, she leaped into action. She triggered a chain of tactical maneuvers, a deployment of sorts, whose speed and precision made our dad's clumsily concealed indulgences look like a clown car circus act. My mother extracted herself, and us by extension, from the precarities of her most important relationship by staging a midnight coup, an operation she carried out with special-ops-level stealth and covert logistics. Overnight, she called a locksmith to attend to the front door of our house, which was seldom even closed during warmer months and had never really required a key. We knew from our own wayward moments that when our mother crossed her arms and pursed her lips, you could beg and cry all you wanted, but there was no penance, no crawling back or any kind of saying sorry. There was just no talking her out of it. It was as if she'd been masterminding your punishment for years and was merely waiting for your final slip-up to arrive. At that point, all you could do was pray, even if praying had never been your thing.

If it blew our mother's hair back to excavate this fiscal infidelity, then it blindsided nobody more than our dad, who'd dug the hole with the breezy je ne sais quoi of a pot-smoking teenager at an open-air music festival. He'd believed in money as an endlessly renewable resource and, as such, never really hid his illiquid habits. There was no wrongdoing a man could perpetrate with the contents of his own wallet. He thought the heyday would last forever—until the end of forever arrived.

Our father's wrath had always seemed so blustery and fearsome, but it paled in comparison to our mother's when she really put her foot down, and he rolled over and accepted it, too stunned to do much more than acquiesce. My dad, who'd always been testy and temperamental, capitulated without too much of a fight. Maybe he believed in the total resilience of the family, that our house could withstand any tornado. Perhaps he thought our mother was incapable of making good on her threats. Or maybe it was just the way he experienced life, in the high times of the goldfish ever-present, never truly committing to the uncertainties of tomorrow until they finally showed up. But possibly he accepted this ultimate severance as a form of relief, the way desperados lie down for the handcuffs when the cops finally bust down the door. Perhaps he, too, had been expecting it all along, waiting for the hammer to drop so he could have what he'd subconsciously desired all along, release from a life that he'd only half chosen, which had been shaped as much by accidental luck as unfortunate, involuntary circumstances.

He packed his Corvette with few belongings, mostly because his car had no real cargo space. We knew he traveled light because our house remained almost exactly the same, with not a stick of furniture or a piece of cutlery out of place, so that all that was missing was his corporeal presence plus the many linear feet of his wardrobe. It was as if he'd returned to the unencumbered state of his London days—in a way, a full circle.

After this banishment, he slunk away to a motel on the highway outside of town where it was hard to imagine any-

one staying unless they were in similarly blighted circumstances. We visited him there a few times, but his weakened,
vulnerable state was hard to witness, as if all his power had
derived from us, his next of kin, and the nest from which
he'd fallen. The force that governed all our lives had been so
quickly deactivated. These visits were complicated by the
fact that two of his kids had learner's permits requiring adult
driver supervision, and our mother couldn't stand to be
within firing distance of her future former spouse. It was all
too much to bear, our dad sitting on a polyester bedspread,
watching a janky TV. A king on a broken throne, wearing a
cockeyed crown.

Several weeks passed after the split. From the motel, our
dad continued to work at the town hospital, but everything
had changed. Where once he was heavy as a thundercloud,
now he became light as a cirrus wisp. Soon he drifted off,
almost as easily as he'd disappeared from our house in the
first place. He moved away to a new city. My dad never
found another place to live in our town, if he ever tried.
That wasn't his way. His mode, when he'd finished with
something, was to get up and move along. He seldom turned
back. He looked ahead to the horizon, where the sun was
still shining.

IT WAS LIKE waking up from a deep, strange dream. It was
impossible to see what had been lost or gained in the after-
math.

Everyone in town seemed to know what had happened
to us almost before my dad had finished packing. People
talked because we lived in a small place, but also because
they owed my dad no debt of respect or privacy, possibly

because he'd sauntered around our hardworking little village like Rich Uncle Pennybags, possibly because he'd skipped town with an open tab at many a local restaurant, at least the ones with surf and turf and flambéed fruit on the menu. Our mother never cared at all what people had to say, but she'd always been private. She wanted no one's pity, nor their schadenfreude, our doctor-mother with her die-hard British accent and precious little time for chitchat at the grocery store. As a newly reduced family unit, we stopped going out for dinner entirely, except to joints that served drinks in waxed paper cups and french fries in Styrofoam clamshells. And nobody was sad, at least not about the loss of fancy food. As it turned out, we all preferred hoagie sandwiches and picnics in the car and root beer guzzled straight from the can.

In the after-times, our mother fell into a somnambulistic period of divorcée recovery. She seemed relieved and lighter, more ready to laugh at our jokes, but she also slept like the dead, as if finally released from the stressful vigilance of her prior marital life. On weekend mornings, she couldn't be woken with a door knock or even a gentle touch on the shoulder. When nudged, she'd wake with a groggy start, as if from the anesthesia she dosed out to patients each day.

Many things became bracingly clear, some of them for the first time in our tiny, cosseted lives. First of all, we discovered what life was like in a single-parent household. Although our dad had never contributed in the standard way, not as an American breadwinner might, he was gone now. There was only one person in the world to protect and shield us, to watch over our growth and progress. We were one human adult away from being all on our own, which was perhaps the way it had always really been.

Now our mother could parent however she liked, exactly
as she saw fit, without anyone else's input. If we were close
to the finish line of childhood, the split had pushed us the
rest of the way. She started to talk to us, her elder kids, in
ways she never had before. We had many conversations
about the family disintegration along with the attendant
outcomes. How to start over, we wondered? How to find the
way forward? I peppered her with many questions, practical
and existential. Did he care what happened to us now that
we were absent from his direct line of sight? Would he come
to our graduation?

She shielded us from our dad's naked facts, but the con-
verse was also true. She was protecting him from us and our
resentments, which had snowballed long before the split and
would surely endure into the future. But there was no way
to explain what had happened to our family without at least
some watered-down dose of the truth. In many ways, we
needed no explanation at all. We were well aware of our
dad's resplendent personality. He hadn't left for nothing.
We'd always known him as a man with wandering attentions. He couldn't make it through a dish of pasta without
allowing his fork to drift over to someone else's plate.
Watching TV with him was a dizzying experience, a whirl-
ing montage of talking heads and sitcom fragments, half-
finished slap shots and free throws interrupted in midair.
Just as my eyeballs attuned to each channel, he'd flick on to
the next. Now our house was cluttered with his castaway
technologies, the exotic antennae and rabbit ears he'd
bought in the pre-cable days so he could poach the *Hockey
Night in Canada* signal from the other side of the border.
Our father's wavering loyalty had always been an open secret. But that was just one reason.

He was an intelligent man, undoubtedly so. How could he have deep-sixed the very things he'd worked so hard to build—an immigrant's bonanza, the great, prosperous family pie in the sky—unless that had been his unconscious wish all along? Unless there was no other way he knew how to be, no training that might have taught him otherwise. His errors seemed to boil down to one misbelief, enacted again and again in a thousand iterations. It expressed itself in the style with which he entered his own home, the way he moved through our shared air. He removed his shoes and dropped them from a height in the foyer. He took a hand towel from its rod and dried his fingers but didn't return it to the original place, as if that square of household linen had been waiting for him to come home and make use of it. When our mother was down with a cold, he became sympathetically sick with the sniffles. He took over the kitchen table with a bowl of steaming water, his head tented over it by yet another towel. If he was peckish, he stood before the fridge with the door wide open waiting for something tasty to show itself from behind the Velveeta or grape jelly. His place in our house was a nonnegotiable tenure, a forever-job that couldn't ever be changed, shaken, or lost. He'd wrongly assumed those powers were absolute, even beyond the envelope of his native culture. On the west side of the Greenwich meridian, he'd taken his blessings for granted.

Our mother had stayed with our dad for Catholic reasons, the sanctity of the family, the sacrament of the union, etc., etc. But that wasn't the whole story. Maybe she'd succumbed to a sunk-cost fallacy. Or worse, she'd stayed not for herself but for us, a sacrifice far too squidgy and terrible to contemplate directly. She didn't have any close friends nearby, no one she could trust with her recent calamities.

Now she was all alone with three children, stuck in a country without family or support, with nobody to listen but an old man priest with dodgy, sidelong eyes. Wasn't this like being dropped overboard in the middle of the sea, in some ways harder and more uncertain than weathering an uncomfortable marriage?

My parents' split signaled the end of my oblivion, especially when it came to economics. I became aware of our mother's financial burdens. Our father had squeezed her dry of more than just patience. He'd raided the family coffers for all they were worth and beyond, and now there was nothing left but arrears. This must have been a heartbreak to our mother with two kids so close to their postsecondary years. She'd been the first person in her family to go to college, her biggest leap forward in life. But now we were just like everybody else, all those folks who'd been dazzled by the dream—overspent, overfed, divorced, and beyond broke. Now we were truly Americans.

On the plus side, it was also a Mardi Gras of newfound teenage freedom. My brother and I felt like calves sprung into the pasture after a long, dark winter in the barn. After our father's departure, the house took on a new kind of life. Nobody was afraid of open chatter or laughter anymore. Our house filled with my friends and my brother's friends so that there was hardly a silent moment, which confounded our little sister, who was a sensitive introvert even as a primary school kid, never seen without a book in her hand. She looked up from her pages to contemplate our traffic as if we were a herd of wildebeests stampeding through.

All the things I'd never been allowed to do suddenly became available in luxuriant profusions. My only impediment to the unfettered use of the phone was competition for airtime with my brother. We could play our music as loud as we liked, and our mother never complained. In fact she often asked what we were listening to, curious about the strange new sounds wafting around her house. I could come and go as a regular teenager without dekeing like a fugitive around the spotlight of my dad's watchful eye. She didn't care if I dressed like a fool in a miniskirt in the frigid depths of winter. She didn't care if I wore blue eyeliner and frosted brown lipstick to school. Could she overlook it if we borrowed her car and snuck off to Quebec to buy beer? Could I go to swim camp in the next town over? Could she forgive me if I stayed out late getting up to no good with my friends? She'd think about it for a minute or two, then give in. Why not? Everything had been "no" for so long, why not let it be "yes" for once?

In the time that had elapsed since my dad had left home, I'd found a couple of part-time jobs. I was a lifeguard at the pool for early-bird swims. I went before school to watch over old ladies in flowered bathing caps as they paddled back and forth in the same lanes where I trained during afternoon practices, bashing out thousands of cathartic yards. I got a job teaching a seniors' aerobics class at the local gym, despite my total lack of skill or qualifications in that department. Even so, the overarching themes were the same. I supervised people's everyday strivings, their quiet efforts to get better, healthier, or happier, which felt like a totally different way to improve than the one my dad always reached for. His methods looked like dazzle, drama, and flyaway dollar bills. They shuttled between fireworks and self-sabotage.

My dad, who'd been such a force of nature in our little world, the source of all our most piercing emotions, lifted up and blew away, leaving in his wake an unsettling vacuum

of calm the likes of which we'd never experienced before.
No spasms of Pavlovian panic when his car rolled up in the
driveway. No sound of his keys jangling. We didn't have to
tiptoe around on Saturday mornings for fear of waking him
up. It felt almost like a regular American house. And although we no longer had to duck into the shrubbery or slip
out through the garage whenever he came home, we could
hear ourselves think for the first time. I wasn't sure I really
knew what to do with the silence.

LONG PERIODS ELAPSED between dad sightings. He moved
down to Houston, where his sister resided, his closest North
American relative. She lived in the suburbs with our uncle
and cousins in a traditional Indian household, at least when
compared to ours. Their house was seldom quiet or empty,
since it was often home to a rotating cast of extended family
members in need, or friends from afar who'd come to town
for medical attention.

Our father never returned to our little hamlet in New
York State. Instead, we went to stay with him during our
summer vacations or winter holiday breaks from school.
These trips involved sibling configurations that sometimes
included my sister, but often enough my twin and I flew
down together, unaccompanied by our mother, since many
years would have to pass before they could meet without
somebody turning to salt. These were the sorts of parental
visits endured by thousands, probably millions, of other
kids—at least the ones with maintenance orders and separation agreements in effect. Our fathers were single dads, living solo for the first time all over again, watching football
alone, cracking bottles of Michelob and bags of cheese puffs

for dinner, finally, because nobody was watching or asking them to set a good example. They enjoyed the liberty they didn't really want anymore, not for the heavy price they'd paid.

In his new Houston life, our dad appeared stripped of the comforts and the organizational padding of his former domestic life. This is what he looked like with our mother cut away, as if she had been the force holding him together all along. He now lived in a condo, low-slung and dark, a slightly more down-market version of the bachelor grotto he occupies today. His unit had bare beige walls and nothing in the cupboards but Planters peanuts and an assortment of plastic takeout forks, as if he expected to depart again at any moment. Beyond that, not much about his habits had changed. He drove an even flashier used car despite his purportedly empty wallet, a two-seater Porsche, which presented all the familiar problems when it came to the transportation of his offspring. Either my brother or I sat comfortably in the front while the other contorted into the back-seat compartment, which had no seatbelts and wasn't really a seat at all.

My dad didn't actually know how to manage kids on his own; he'd never really learned how. Our visits to his house sometimes transformed into stays with our aunt, who lived a few suburbs away from my dad, close enough for connection, but too far for invasions of privacy or disapproving glimpses into his lifestyle. When we stayed with him, he went to work with no modifications to his schedule, so we hung around the apartment, or were visited by middle-aged women strangers with nice nails and immaculate grooming who also drove impractical sports cars, his new friends presumably, to entertain us during business hours. We went to

Galveston Island, not to the beach or the state park, as our mother would have chosen, but to adult tourist destinations, shopping strands with jewelry boutiques and gift stores, the kinds of places you'd go if you didn't know anything about kids, or if you were constrained by walking around in high heels.

My dad made little mention of the events that had befallen us. And we acted like nothing had changed, too, mostly because the change was obvious to all involved. We pretended not to know that our mother had been barraging him, rather futilely, with legal reminders. We faked the ongoing myth of soaring uplift in our now-divided lives, partly because he appeared so crumpled and beaten down about the edges. We faked it to preserve his dignity, but also because we didn't want to talk about this hot mess to which we belonged that was not of our making, at least not directly, not in ways that were easy to admit.

When I arrived at my dad's house, I began counting down the days until I could leave. I didn't exactly enjoy his company—that was nothing new. But I also felt worse for him than ever before, since now his loneliness was palpable, and this also felt like ours to carry. The whole package was wrapped in a layer of obligation, since these weren't just visits, they were visitation rights. The more we tried to escape togetherness, the more enforced it became.

In his world, nothing made any real sense. He lived in a rental unit and drove a high-end gas guzzler, but besides that, he had not much to show for his decades of striving but a bunch of double-breasted suits in plastic dry-cleaning bags. He seemed possessed by a bent for destruction of all that he'd built, as if that's where he felt most comfortable, at the start of the dream rather than its conclusion, where there was nowhere to go but up.

My brother and I were just months away from leaving home. We had no idea where to go or how to get there now that our former life paths, assigned to us from birth, had disappeared in the tall grass. We had no parent stable enough, without a quagmire of their own to manage, to tell us what to do. I'd taken my mother's side for most of my adolescence, but even that was overtaken by a craving for structure, for psychic tidiness where none existed except in the future. It felt risky to know my father, to let him close to my unmade decisions.

On my final visit to my dad's place in Houston, he took my brother and me to an overpriced restaurant with broody lighting where he ordered on my behalf, an off-menu pasta dish, and the chef took his revenge by infusing my dinner with sadistic lashings of hot sauce that paralyzed my taste buds for a few days afterward.

I didn't know this would be the last time I'd visit my father in what was left of his forties, or that it would be the last he'd see of me until I became a full-fledged adult, transformed by all that would happen in the absence. When I think of these last days of my youth spent hanging around my dad's semi-empty apartment, my memory lets go. I can't remember the details, the exact shapes of the rooms, or the strangers I met, or the names of the airlines, or who among my siblings came along at any given time. The whole thing was a muddle, a soup of emotion and cognitive dissonance. My brain refused to hold on to these facts, committing only to shards and glimpses.

When we returned to my dad's place after dinner, I felt

the pressure brewing behind my eyes. Maybe he'd begun to talk, as he often did, of his divorce as an unfortunate event that had befallen him exclusively, accidentally, like a falling pane of office-tower glass. Or maybe he'd sent me off on a feminine kitchen errand, to fetch a Coke as he'd asked me to do so many times before. Perhaps he'd questioned the scores I'd received on my SAT exams after scrutinizing them a little too closely. I don't remember precisely the comment because it was nothing out of the ordinary, nothing I hadn't heard a hundred times and learned to deflect before another one headed my way. He might have chastised me for my no-frills college plans, which I'd executed entirely without his input. I'd sent off a batch of hasty university applications, but none of them landed anywhere close to Cambridge, Ithaca, or New Haven. The Ivy League had been his fantasy, never mine—a pipe dream now, at any rate.

No matter the offhand quip, I could feel the residual heat of my radioactive linguine dinner climbing up the sides of my neck. We'd met our tipping point, my dad and me, and the balance had shifted in my direction. I didn't have to listen to any of his advice or follow his directives. He couldn't demand I do anything; he could only ask and say "please," because now I had claimed the grown child's advantage. I had all the time in the world on my side.

That was *it,* I said. I'd had enough. I couldn't take another minute. If I had to hear another word come out of his mouth, I'd light my own hair on fire.

And then some final cool pond of restraint inside me evaporated, just steamed away. All I could see was white.

ZONES OF ALIENATION

I DIDN'T KNOW ANYTHING ABOUT THE REALITIES OF college life. I'd said "yes" to the first place that accepted me. And then I headed back to Toronto, the city my dad had always refused to revisit, vowing to loathe it until the end of forever, which made it a safe bet for me. But mostly I'd chosen that place because tuition was cheap, and I was thinking of my mother, guilty about the weight I added to her life just when she'd been flattened. That's how I came to leave America, by serendipity and circumstance, according to the family motif.

At the start of classes, I arrived in my hillbilly upstate sweatshirt and acid-wash jeans to a campus that sprawled between neighborhoods and traffic-clogged streets. At the top of every hour, the ivy-covered brick buildings disgorged thousands of young people wearing nineties grunge flannel and torn shorts and long hippie dresses with Doc Martens, more students than the entire population of my little beater town on the upstate fringe of America. A place to get lost in.

I moved into a ramshackle student house, a warren of bedrooms and a kitchen with three refrigerators crammed with chocolate milk, takeout leftovers, and wilted, vintage vegetables. Here I hauled my twin-sized futon up the steps to a small room on the second floor whose window over-looked an alleyway, following in the footsteps of thousands of students who'd come before me.

Our house had a gray common room that looked like the set of an existentialist play with its boxy, abused sofa and a small TV in the corner. My roommates and I crammed in to watch the fall of the Berlin Wall, an edifice whose solidity had once seemed permanent, just as the childhoods and family lives at our backs had once seemed solid and un-changeable. The news streamed footage of thousands of young people partying in the streets, clambering over barri-cades, and dancing on the Brandenburg Gate with frothing beer cans in their fists. These kids were our age, but they'd lived their whole lives in the shadow of the wall. And just like that, the immovable past became part of the future. A thing we thought would last forever was over in a day.

In the drafty student house, I made several instant friends. And then I made even more friends in the wide-open world of campus, populated as it was by hordes of fellow under-graduates flowing in and out of gigantic classes. In their company I quickly realized I was a sheltered hayseed, pain-fully oblivious to the features of my new urban lifestyle. I endured their gentle ridicule for my vowel-murdering up-state accent and patient teasing for all the things I didn't know. I pronounced "falafel" all wrong because I'd never tried it before. I'd grown up in a place without "ethnic" food beyond the accidental fusion cuisine we ate at home. My new city friends had to stop me from consuming whole knobs of wasabi in the sushi takeout. I had not heard of Superchunk or Sonic Youth or Dinosaur Jr. or any of the music they listened to. I had never seen grown men with long, flowing hair walk right down the street as if they'd stepped from Herbal Essences commercials.

Freedom was exhilarating, like a portal to another dimension. It gave me the feeling of existing outside myself, as if my brain had not yet caught up with my body in space and time. I'd spent years just trying to get around my dad's eagle eye. Now I was reading campus bathroom posters with tips on how to avoid getting roofied at the bar. Here they gave away condoms by the fistful.

I learned to expect the old, familiar hatch of origin questions. Whenever I walked into a new seminar or a party full of strangers it wasn't long before someone asked me what I was, what ethnic ingredients had made me. I no longer lived in a little town where everyone already knew the answer. I saw that I'd probably have to field this question until the end of my days, or the next Halloween party, whatever came first. The realization jingled like a little reminder bell in the back of my head: I could try to avoid it all I wanted, but there was no running away from my own skin.

Toronto had changed a lot in the years since we'd lived there as a family, at least it looked that way beyond the streets of the monotone suburb where we'd lived all those years ago. On the subway and on the sidewalks, everywhere I looked, there were faces in every shade from ruddy pink to light beige to deep brown. In a city with a phone book full of Johals and Singhs and Gills, I saw a lot of people whose eyebrows and nose shapes I recognized, whose turbans I spotted from half a block away. I looked at them, and they looked at me, often in mild puzzlement, unable to decide where and if I belonged among them. But in my corner of campus, it was still largely white, at least in the humanities, an almost purposefully vague area of study where no self-respecting tiger parent would ever let their kid stray, not even for elective purposes.

I submerged in this pool without any trouble at all. I'd grown up in similar spaces, and I knew very well how to fold myself into a crowd, especially when the crowd was homogenized. I'd gotten used to occupying one side of my halfsie body for reasons that felt more emotional than po-litical. I'd aligned with my mother, had grown fiercely pro-tective of her interests. It was also my way of distancing myself from my father, whom I'd not seen since that last time I'd visited him in Texas. It had been months since we'd spoken.

I decided to enroll as an English major. It had always been my secret leaning, and now it became my open inten-tion, especially since I knew my father would receive this like a crime against humanity. Any discipline outside STEM was, according to him, "useless." Even my mother hesitated over my choice, worried it would prepare me for a well-read life of penury. She was also science-based, not to mention a born-again believer in women's liquidity. But she'd always been a pushover, especially without my dad around to act as bad cop. What was the point of paying tuition, I argued, to study something I couldn't stand and wasn't good at? She came around to the idea that one's actual interests might factor into an education, whereas my dad believed nothing should be left up to anyone before age thirty, even opinions, lest anarchy break out in the streets and society crumble into zombie oblivion. So I never told him about it. It was just one more thing I shoved into the silent zone between us.

IT OCCURRED TO me late in that first semester that English Literature did not mean reading novels for fun. Englit featured the collected narratives of England, inescapably so, everything from Chaucer to Martin Amis and all the historical periods in between. It was written mostly by middle-aged men of the leisure class who meditated on the waterfalls of the Alps or obsessed over unavailable women or observed wars from the sidelines. These dry meringues of studied beauty were taught by white faculty in seminar rooms and lecture halls and occasionally in the pews of the university chapels whose stained glass I stared up at during lectures. It was the most time I'd ever spent in churches thinking about God, the afterlife, and paradise lost or gained.

Despite my parents' continental foundations, my education thus far had been parochial, even primitive compared to my classmates', many of whom had done an extra year of college prep. My parents had been taught grammar and math by rote, had memorized encyclopedic amounts of history. For them, stellar marks equaled a stellar education. But I did not yet know how to write a college paper, or how to find a book in a fourteen-story research library. In the schools of my youth, I'd learned to baste raw edges in sewing class and learned to type on an electric Smith Corona. I knew extensive facts regarding the three branches of the U.S. government and had practically memorized *The Catcher in the Rye,* but I didn't really know how to learn. I studied just like a high school student, hard but indiscriminately, with no sense of triage or strategy, as if wading headlong across a fast-flowing river when the footbridge was right around the corner.

I committed to my slog through the centuries of Anglo-Saxon literary grandeur, but it wasn't until *Frankenstein, Middlemarch,* and *Emma* in the intermediate years of my degree that the pot finally began to boil. The perspective of these lady novelists differed from the gentleman poets whose mental space I'd been sharing since the start of my studies. These women authors didn't really concern themselves with the chiming of the spheres or the marriages of heaven and hell. They turned their gazes toward earthly practicalities, relationships, emotions, commitments, entrapments. There was something tentative about their interrogations. They were less sure than their male contemporaries. They posed many of the same questions I'd been asking myself since the first day I'd put on a bra. How to make the best of one's brief comet ride through the vapors? How to satisfy the hungers of the mind while living within the constraints of expectation? How to exist in one world while also living beside it—next to it but not of its making? In this way they gave shape to something that was otherwise invisible, a scaffolding of sorts, the way dew reveals a cobweb.

With every year, a fresh epiphany. In the later phases of my undergraduate schooling, I dipped into the mysterious theory-speak of deep academe with its hegemonies and dialectics, its Freudian interpretations amid Marxist philosophies weighed against feminist critiques. I fell in with a small cadre of lit-crit dorks who said things like, "Do you mean difference, or is it *différance?*"

They said, "Everybody knows Valter Benyamin. Haven't we all read Valter Benyamin to death by now?" I had not read Walter Benjamin. I had not done anything to death. I was just getting started.

Then I came across the work of Edward Said, whose voice rang like a clear bell in a field of garbled noise. He was a Palestinian living in exile, but he was also American. He was both those things at the same time. He'd read the canon just as I was doing, but he didn't take these works at face value. He considered this literature not just as art or entertainment, but as artifacts that confessed a secret. The secret involved a way of seeing and believing. It belonged to everyone and no one all at once. The bards of Europe, no matter their talents or purported objectivity, were dipped in a certain sensibility, a way of looking at the rest of the world, the East in particular. They had a way of seeing the very people they'd colonized as crude and poor, exotic yet prone to barbarism, patriarchal yet sexually submissive, untainted by change or history, therefore reliant upon imperial saviors for the gifts of technology and civilization. They overwrote these people with the sheer volume and conviction of their output.

For Said, there was no literature without politics, no narrative without power. These things were all stirred together so that one could not be extracted from the other. Orientalism wasn't an anachronism or a fad. It was everywhere, pervading all the movies I'd watched as a kid, all the TV shows that taught me to be an American. It flowed through everything I'd read at university, even the way it was curated and taught. The very halls where I learned and studied were also instruments of its force. And somehow this acknowledgment made sense of everything, tied it all together, even if I couldn't tease apart all the threads. It gave me the feeling of climbing a mountain, of gaining elevation and perspective on the valleys from which I'd come.

By then I'd dabbled in an area called Commonwealth Literature, stories from the territories of the Empire, which I'd discovered with some dismay was not always written by natives of those countries but rather by émigrés with sunburns and a shared fondness for white linen and pith helmets. But this was changing. That literary turf was slowly infiltrated by immigrated writers of the former colonies, many of whom wore jeans and lived in New York and London, but whose books looked secondhand even when they were brand-new. These titles came with sepia-toned jackets featuring fog and smoke, overripe mangos, and sari borders, perfectly preserved worlds that existed nostalgically in the past, as if in wish fulfillment for a simpler time, or a world that stayed forever as it was before the people fought back, before the tourists showed up, with oxcarts and cobbled streets, like a little colonial theme park.

By the time I hit the fourth year, all the titles I'd binge-read and slogged through—all the plays and poems and novels and manifestos—became something more than the sum of their parts. They felt like patches of awareness that grew and expanded, until eventually those pieces began to touch upon one another, to intersect and overlap, until finally a pattern was suggested. In this way, I saw that education was important, but not for the reasons my dad had suggested. Learning could be a privilege, and it could be a quietly radical act in its knowledge-borrowing and intel-sharing. Why else deny it to certain people, my grandmothers among them? Education had power, and once I'd had a taste, there was no way of unknowing it, no way to force it back into the bottle. And that alone was worth the price of entry to the useless pursuit of the arts.

DURING THOSE UNIVERSITY years, I didn't see my father even once, a semi-deliberate choice, possibly for us both. I didn't have the strength to keep arguing with him while also breaking trail for myself, which gave me a taste of how he must have felt when he was my age, floating about Europe all on his own. I knew where he lived, and I kept his number, but every time I looked at the phone, I just couldn't bring myself to do it. I never called him, and he never called me. I knew his reasons, same as always; it was up to me to show filial piety, to do the dirt-eating work of patching things over, according to the old-world ways of parent and child.

My brother drifted from our father as well. He joined the military, and whatever need he'd had for a role model was replaced by the army's hypermasculine paradigm of love and sacrifice. Through most of my twenties, the only person who really saw my father was our little sister, but eventually, when she got old enough, she'd fall out with him, too.

My mother pulled herself slowly from the crater. She sold the gray house on the misspelled street, barely breaking even. She found another place closer to work, way out in the country, where nobody knew or cared about her marital tribulations. Eventually, once my little sister graduated from high school and shipped out to university, our mother would pull up stakes and move into a humble little house in a new town on the Canadian side of the border. She'd never felt like an American, she said. "That was your father's idea."

After my brother and I flew the nest, we had no heartfelt

home to return to, which began a period of drift. We seldom gathered as a family for holidays or birthdays in that post-nuclear decade. With my dad's departure, we lived like a floating constellation of semi-attached individuals, as if our father's many challenges had been the glue that had held us all together. It was the longest I'd spent away from my brother, which felt strange but also liberating, since our childhoods had been unavoidably intertwined; we'd fought this togetherness at many turns, and yet we shared so much perspective. We needed time alone, a kind of privacy, to comb it through.

In the army, Alex graduated from ranger training and chiseled himself into a high-performance human widget. I'd done my own civilian version of the same thing. In the summer months between semesters, I worked as a tree-planter, which took me north in Canada to the boreal forest, or what was left of it, before it had been converted by clear-cut logging into an industrial wasteland. I didn't mind this landscape, despite its ecological tragedies. It was about as far as I could get, existentially speaking, from my dad's way of life.

On the job, entirely different things were demanded of me. I had to learn to work in rain, hail, and snow all day and then sleep in a tent whose nylon walls flapped and sagged beneath those same elements. Each tree was worth seven cents, and everybody got paid the same rate. No specialty, no exceptions, no five-star service. Nobody cared what I looked like, if my hands were dirty, if I was a girl, or if I was white or brown, or what school I went to, or my family pedigree, or any other form of social distinction. I spent long days walking among the tree stumps, bashing away at the earth with my rusty shovel in the birdless quiet of the clear-cuts, and despite the physical devastations of the experience, there was a soothing, gritty blankness to it, which after the marginally controlled mayhem of my youth came as a long-awaited relief.

My college graduation came and went, but I never attended the ceremony. I was done with formalities, with exams and assessments of all kinds. I was on my own now, under nobody's watch. It was time to be someone else, time to take on the preposterous task of finding a job in recessionary times armed with not much more than an arts degree, an expired lifeguard ticket, and an ability to tolerate inclement weather in a T-shirt. I moved to British Columbia, about as far west as one could go without falling into the ocean, and then I went back to work as an outdoor schlep, this time with no good reason to leave, no aspirational semesters to return to. I departed for work in the mornings smelling of dryer sheets and returned at night stippled in mud from head to toe, my cheeks crusted with sweat. After a thousand days spent bent grubbing in the fields and a thousand more to go, I didn't get why my parents were so afraid of dirty jobs. It was my luxury never to know. In the winters, I worked as a secretary. I made coffee and photocopies and spreadsheets for men in suits who didn't know I existed, not as a real person. But I didn't really care. I'd been pelted by every kind of precipitation, yelled at by foremen. I'd tripped and fallen countless times. But none of those things were as terrible as my parents had promised; they felt neutral, impersonal to me. They felt like the consequences of the choices I'd made for myself on the path to elsewhere.

I'd also started roaming around with the same itchy wanderlust that had afflicted my parents. For the rest of my twenties, I'd spend many months wearing a backpack, tearing spent pages from the spines of *Lonely Planet* guidebooks, beating my passport to a sweaty, worn pulp. Sometimes I'd buy a plane ticket on the first day of my off-season, and then I'd jet away, sometimes in the company of boyfriends, often on my own.

I kept in touch with my mother by phone no matter where I found myself. She applauded my travels, but she also worried about me, hoping I'd discover the benefits of settling down along with the secrets of compound interest. She'd been burned that one time. But this was the way I'd been raised, I pointed out, without any staying powers. I'd discovered—just as my parents had—that something could be found, or perhaps escaped, in the rush of takeoff, even if it was temporary at best.

IT TOOK ME quite a while to get to India. For years, other countries kept getting in the way. I wanted to go, but I didn't want to go, at least not to explore my roots, at least not seriously, since no one from the family had lived there for two generations. But still that country held magnetic appeal in my imagination, as if something might be found there. I intended to spend a few months touring forts and temples with some heavy gustatory sightseeing on the side. But I didn't find what I'd expected, not exactly.

My first day in India, I woke up in a budget hotel room in Mumbai to the sound of gagging just beyond my door. This noise was alarming and yet strangely familiar to me. I peeked out into the hallway to see what the trouble was about and discovered a woman in a turquoise sari and a lot of tinkling jewelry hunched over the hallway sink. She held her braid in one hand and a toothbrush in the other, and when I emerged, she stood up and smiled at me with her mouth full of white foam. This was the way my dad brushed his teeth, loud and proud, as if he were trying to scrub his uvula along with his furthermost molars.

I moved without a fixed itinerary. Over my months on the subcontinent I found myself drawn not to the ashrams or the beaches of Goa or the Taj Mahal, but to the north with its little villages and crumbling ruins, the abandoned cities of ancient empires, as if I'd been tugged there by the pages of an E. M. Forster novel, on the hunt for something that could no longer be found, or that had never been real to begin with.

Everywhere I traveled I saw glimmers of my dad's tics and patterns. The way he pushed a torn chapati around on a plate. The way he drank water, on rare hydration occasions, by pouring it from a short height directly into his mouth, without any lip-to-vessel contact. The way he wore his woolen scarves like a patient with the mumps, over the top of his head, then tied beneath the chin. My dad was very particular about his tea rituals, insistent that this beverage be piping hot and not too strong, with milk, never cream, plus a small dump truck of sugar. Every chai wallah I visited, no matter the rickety stall or the roadside bus stop, was also fastidious about the temperature, the perfect cleanliness of the cup, the appropriate level of dairy, the attendant froth of the product.

Indian males weren't afraid of boisterous fashions. They shared an easy bodily affection for one another. Young men held hands platonically on the streets, slung their arms over each other's shoulders. Kissing between men and women was censored out of Bollywood movies, even for married characters. It was still taboo for couples to touch in public. But outdoor intimacy was A-okay for men, which explained a lot about my dad's preference for male company.

Even my dad's handwriting looked Indian to me once I'd been to India.

It occurred to me—an obvious, late-breaking realization—that there were parts of him that had been inspired by the country of his birth to which he'd never returned. He knew it only by proxy, yet still it informed so much of his life. If he'd been with me, rambling around the streets of Delhi or Varanasi, he might have shared my revelation. "Look at that," he'd have said with his hands on his hips, shaking his head in amazement. How similar, how familiar this world was, its cultures old and powerful, like déjà vu or a recurring dream.

India felt like the opposite of buttoned-down, beige North America with its rampant individualism lurking just beneath. In India's bustling streets, somehow my dad's maximalist tendencies made a strange kind of sense. There was no such thing as overdoing it. There was always room for more. Another little bit to share. Another butt on the bench. Another body in the train car until one was touched on all sides by one's fellow earthlings. How else might a billion people fit with such timeless efficiency into a single country? There was no such thing as too much, only moving over to make a little more room.

No matter where I went, alone or in the company of fellow travelers I met along the way, one thing remained the same. I couldn't go far without the same old questions, just in different format. Nobody mistook me for a local, but there was always curiosity about my near-Indian looks. The farther north I traveled, the closer to the homeland, the truer this became.

"Looking like India?"

"Little bit India?"

Almost everywhere I went, I met extended family units traveling all together—babies, parents, grandparents— multiple branches of the tree moving as one to weddings, festivals, the houses of other relatives. They had questions for me, too. Why was I alone? Where was my family? Over and over again.

In the backward-facing logic of hindsight, our family's dissolution seemed inevitable, from start to finish. When I laid out the misfit parts of our hinky machine, it felt kind of outrageous to me that it had worked at all, let alone run smoothly. The real miracle was that we'd stayed together for as long as we had, or that anyone had dared to attempt it in the first place. Such were the optimisms of the freshly arrived and the reinventors of the wheel.

I misunderstood my parents for many years, especially my father. I couldn't see him in his human totality, couldn't register that he was just a tiny footnote in a larger saga cast over broad geographies and big spreads of time. I didn't understand that we were a cup poured into a tide of generational wavelets, people leaving and starting over, each paying the toll in a new world by giving up a little bit of the old one. And I, too, formed a part of this current as its farthest ripple, deposited on the shore without ever knowing how the surge had originated.

WHAT IS A grudge but an argument plus pride and time? Mine had a shape, an arc, a lifespan all its own. It had been ten years since I'd fallen out with my father, the halfway point in our estrangement. I came back to Canada and moved into a tiny apartment in Vancouver. I hatched plans to go back to school to study the fine art of writing—possibly the worst vocational outcome to a brown immigrant dad, which I noted with a certain degree of objective amusement.

But then my feelings about my father morphed into a kind of curiosity. My mother and I began to talk about him again, bitching on the phone about his foibles, joking about his many eccentricities that we'd survived. He was a hard person to be mad at forever.

"Do you think he ever thinks about us?" I asked. Did he wonder how we were?

"No," she said. She didn't think he did.

She may have been right, but I also knew my dad well—beneath all his testy intemperance, he had a soft, emotional center.

All kinds of life transpired in our gap, as I'd come to think of it. My twenties gave way to my thirties. I went to grad school. I settled down on the west coast. I continued the grub work of planting trees. I wrote my first book. I met my husband and we got married, another event my dad missed because he hadn't been invited. I was still my father's daughter, but I was a new person, too. I could remember the feelings I'd had, but not their rawness or intensity. I'd been molten on the inside, but after the lava cooled, my feelings transformed. I gave the past a little more rope, and although I could still feel the tug of its weight, it dragged behind me at quite a distance. And then one day, in the midst of my thirties, a pivot. I stopped looking back and trained my eyes on our days ahead, which I always knew were numbered.

PART 2

SOMETHING TO DECLARE 12

TO ENTER MY DAD'S MODERN UNIVERSE, FIRST I MUST fly from my little Canadian village to Vancouver in a small, turbulence-prone commuter plane he refers to as "a flying toothpaste tube." My trans-border flights always leave before dawn, so I stay overnight in the Holiday Inn Expresses and the budget airport Travelodges that I know would offend his sensibilities. In these hotel rooms I watch reality TV while shoveling back takeout, both misdemeanors in his books. Then I set several alarms for an hour that is technically morning but still feels like the belly of the night.

I fall out of bed and into my clothes. Breakfast is a swig of mouthwash. At the airport I feed myself into a herd of sleepy-eyed humanity and then into the lineup that forms before the security gates open for the day. After so many trips, I'm sure I see some of the same people heading to

Texas on our shared route, even if we're traveling for different reasons.

I've flowed through many North American airports en route to my father's house, crossing paths with myriad travelers from all over the world, each with their own unique pigmentary endowments, each with a story that ties them to their ancestry and the long thread of their ethnicity, even if that story is only partially known to them, or not known at all. I notice the kinds of people who lug the suitcases and wear the neck pillows and the kinds of people who travel light. The ones who push the mops, who wear the hairnets and hurl the luggage, who chatter among themselves behind the counter at Tim Hortons. The people for whom the automatic faucets turn on and the people for whom they do not. I see who gets to wear the bulletproof vests versus the security-guard pinnies, who wields the sidearms versus the glowing runway batons. Many of them are my father's people, and by extension, they are my people.

Few long-distance travelers are immune to airports unless you're the chartered one percent. Everyone's here. Some people wear cowboy hats and belt buckles. Some wear diamond earring studs and Louis Vuitton handbags. Some people sport the symbolism of home with glorious abandon, without feeling the need to adapt or blend in. I notice who is in priority lanes, who is military. Who asserts their rights to the business-class queues, and who gets the looks when they stand up, too. Who drinks chardonnay at the wine bars and who eats chili fries out of plastic baskets. I note the travelers bound for Frankfurt, London, and Sydney, and the ones destined for Tampa, El Paso, and Lafayette, Louisiana. As with bees in a hive, we're not just a mass of bodies moving in random vibration. There must be some kind of order to it, a pattern.

Airports are uncomfortable. They're ill-designed for sleeping or any other kind of cushy, extended stay. They keep us moving, a river of people with no ties to one another but the shared hope of reaching our separate destinations. We're also a captive audience, melting our credit cards a little along the way. Airport concourses are blandly anonymous—buffed tiles, stainless steel, industrial carpet, inoffensive public art. Their generic sameness makes us forget the vulnerability of the process—we're corralled, funneled down chutes, our bodies scanned, our belongings searched. We have little control over our destinies for all the storms and crew malfunctions, not to mention the customs checks and immigration roadblocks, the uncertainties of foreignness faced by many. We could miss our ultimate connections.

Still, I don't mind the airport because it contains so many possibilities and directions. In theory, you could change your mind at any given moment. You could trade your destination for a new one practically anywhere else in the world. You could flee your old life in a departure-lounge epiphany, just as characters do in rom-coms and political thrillers. I can slingshot myself across light-years of societal existence. I can leave home, where same-sex marriage was legalized twenty years ago, and fly to a state where the death penalty is still carried out semi-regularly. If I merged those two galaxies—here and there—overlapped their dimensions for just a moment, would there be fighting in the streets? Such is the fragile robustness of our civility in the airport. It's the fragile civility of my purpose also. I visit my dad with increasing frequency these days, something I never would have imagined in the years we spent apart—a span exceeding the entirety of my childhood.

There are plenty of layovers on a trip to my dad's, and often I walk the airports in laps just to keep the blood from pooling. My eye is always drawn to interracial couples sitting close or perhaps keeping a distance, or walking as my parents used to, side by side or one just in front of the other, but never holding hands. I notice the mixed-race kids with the mocha complexions, almond eyes, or halos of tightly curled hair. Most of them are decades younger than me. And although they might be too little to understand why, I sometimes wink in their direction. They aren't alone in their mixedness anymore. How do their parents raise them, I wonder, with a tilt to one side or the other? Or do they aim for the straight shot down the middle, if such a thing is possible? Will they one day see their birthright as a blessing or a jinx, or a pearl that coats the grit, the source of the irritation?

Wherever I go, I note the magnetic pull of racial alignment—who lingers in the corners and who moves through the air as if they own it. I'm also searching for something of my own: Where do I fit within this vast chromatic range of human skin? I have never felt totally at ease in my own semi-brown skin, nor with the many labels applied to it. But that's not precisely true. I know exactly the biological materials from which I've been fabricated. Mine is less a crisis of identity than a search for an accurate fit. It's hard to find a niche when we divide ourselves by dark and light, seemingly without the intervening shades of beige.

My true ethnic home is really no place at all. It's a small island nation of the imagination that doesn't exist on any map and not in geologic form. You can't get there via any airport. You can only be born there by fateful accident. Half in and half out, formed from two worlds, belonging to both and neither.

MY DAD PICKS me up at the airport in his red Mercedes as if he's been waiting days for my arrival. I can see that he has from the way he's all dressed up. He's wearing a pair of sand-colored trousers, an aqua short-sleeved shirt, a straw fedora, and a pair of Ray-Ban Aviators that he plucks from his face as soon as he sees me emerge through the sliding doors. He may not be a tall man, but he's never hard to spot.

I step out from the aircon and into a wave of heat. Car windshields glint in the sun, and I have to shield my delicate vampire eyes. He's waiting by his car in the shade of the pickup zone because otherwise the walk is too long, and despite his willingness to drop bank on the finer things, he doesn't like to pay for parking. I make my way over with my battered carry-on in tow, and his face erupts into a smile.

Every time he picks me up at the airport, he looks at me as if newly surprised by my height. In his memory I live as a shorter, younger person. "You've grown," he says. Then he gives me the wooden sideways hug that I've come to associate with senior Indian males, as if they were sworn, at their citizenship ceremonies, to a quota of affectionate North American overshares. My dad looks over my scuffed sneakers, my jeans, and my holey airplane sweater but makes no comment. I hate clothes shopping and can't stand to wear high-maintenance froofery with tight underarms and ironing requirements, and in this, I'm my mother's daughter. But still, I'm delighted to see him, too.

"You must be hungry," he says, more of a statement

than a question. I think he must have a place in mind, some-where he's been waiting to go with company.

"I'm starving," I reply.

He suggests we go out for a very late lunch at a bistro he likes, or a sort-of lunch that involves him watching me in-hale a large quantity of food and bottomless refills of iced tea while he nibbles from the edge of my plate. A lot of the time he eats just once a day, a habit that has followed him from his shifts on the wards and in the operating rooms.

He fills me in on his plotlines. He's been trying to drum up more business for his medical practice. He still works on an extremely part-time basis, reluctant to let go, even though he's well into his eighties, though the looming matter of his retirement is a touchy topic. Then he says he's been feeling cooped up, unable to even leave town because he can't drive for long distances or at night. My dad is a frequent flyer, one of the most extensive roamers I've ever known. Long-haul flights are now risky health-wise, the affronts of modern travel too wearying for a senior citizen's bones.

"You wore out your passport," I say, knowing it bothers him to sit on the bench. My father has several sisters, and he hasn't been able to visit the UK, where they and most of our extended family now live. He hasn't been able to trip around the hotels and restaurants of Europe, one of his favorite places to go, usually on his own, or with the friends he col-lects while holidaying.

Often he reminisces about the trips we've taken together, including all the family vacations when we were still a unit. A few years ago, we went on an Alaska cruise. It rained al-most every day, and I forgot to bring a waterproof coat even though I own several, living as I do in a temperate rainforest. I stood out on the decks in the drizzle, watching whales breach and slap the waves. He wasn't too interested in cetaceans and instead indulged in lavish sleep-ins, which I suppose is anyone's right once they've made it to his age. I spent a lot of time in the hot tub listening to Americans complain openly about all the Chinese families aboard, and then to Australians bitching about the Americans. I explored all the boat's spaces on my hunt for a writing desk with a lovely seafaring aspect, but all I discovered was the sales table of the author-in-residence, who peddled a book called *Wild Life: The Miss-Adventures of a Cosmo Bachelor.*

In Alaska, my dad and I wandered ashore amid the tchotchke shops and faux saloons, then hit the ship's dining rooms for supper. By day three, my dad had fallen in with a group of retirees that included a dentist or a podiatrist, I can't recall. I'm not sure who they were because I never met them. They liked to stay up long past my endurance, long after the closing of the ship's venues, sharing a contraband bottle of Jameson whiskey in the casino's smoking lounge. My dad smelled cooked through with cigar smoke on subsequent days, despite his strenuous assurances that he didn't inhale, he merely sat nearby. No matter the midnight forays, he always woke up cheerful, ready to face another glacier-rimmed afternoon.

But Alaska could never be his natural habitat. He's a person of the world, and while anywhere could be home, no place truly is, not in any root-bound or timeworn way. It's the same way with all of us. We put the nuclear in family. We exploded out all over the map. Each of us now lives in a separate far-flung city.

On the way out of the bistro, I notice my dad's car has

suffered another minor fender bender. This time, the bumper is cracked and scuffed, taped together by someone I struggle to imagine was my dad.

"What happened there?" I ask.

"Don't worry about it," he says, frowning, waving his hand at me, like usual.

This far south, the day is basically as long as the night. The sun disappears without the prelude of a northern twilight, but what it lacks in duration it makes up for in burnt, smudgy brilliance. McAllen is studded with many sand-toned and pink-stuccoed buildings that reflect the blasting subtropical sun, and in the evenings, they light up in the heavy, slantwise glow. It's still warm, the pavement emanating the heat of the day. Flocks of birds are partying in the treetops. This is all a physical relief, as if, back at home in the Great White North, there is a small winter muscle at the back of my neck that contracts every time I open the door. I don't even realize I'm clenching until it relaxes. I left behind the tempestuous weather of Canadian spring, when you can depart in the sun and return in a hail of ice pellets. Or it's windy, or raining sideways. There's always something to face up to.

Later that evening—because my dad refuses to accompany me into such places—I'll stop off at the grocery store to add some chlorophyll and fiber to the everlasting food-like substances he keeps in his refrigerator and cupboards. In this supermarket, there are no dairy cases full of almond milk, no coconut yogurt, no cold-brewed coffee, no super-food smoothies. Shoppers here are unafraid of carbs and saturated fat, just as they don't shy from gluten, animal off-cuts, or the flatulent potential of pinto beans. There are whole aisles devoted to chili peppers and white bread prod-

ucts without an ancient-grain tortilla to be found. Many of
the labels are written in Spanish.

My mother comes from a tall family. I inherited her
height, but even so, on her side I'm one of the shortest at five
feet ten. In the shops of McAllen, occasionally somebody
stops to ask me if I'll reach up to the top shelf to grab a box
or a can beyond their access. Without fail, they are friendly.
And without fail, they address me in Spanish, even though
I'm functionally illiterate in this language. Indeed I have little functionality at all. "No habla," I apologize, caught in
my momentary embarrassment. But then I move on, trolling
the aisles with my basket hooked at my elbow. So much in
this place is unfamiliar to me, and I'm a thousand times a
guest, but this gentle, mistaken hailing has become a regular
experience here, where everyone is my shade of medium
brown, or close to it.

One thing I didn't inherit from my mother is her skin.
She's very fair, with a fine-pored complexion. In winter, her
skin is thirsty and dry. In summer she burns without sun-
screen. I have never once seen her with a pimple or a blem-
ish, whereas my skin is shiny, prone to irritation, in regular
need of depilation. When women say they regret over-
tweezing their brows, I have no idea what they mean. My
hair is Indian—for each one I pull or thread or wax, another
two fight their way back to the surface.

In the pharmacy aisles of South Texas, the shelves are
stocked with skin-enhancing cosmetics in shades of *sun
beige, golden sand,* and *warm honey.* The *vanilla* and the
alabaster are consigned to the neglected bottom racks.
There's not much in the way of self-tanning products, or
color-enhancing conditioners for redheads. The wrinkle
creams take a backseat to the acne treatments. It's all made

and displayed for the ebony-haired and the melanin-equipped, which imparts a tiny glimpse of what it must feel like to be a middle-of-the-road human, just a normal lady back in Canada, the land of blue eyes and blond highlights. In Texas I find every shade of lipstick I could ever want, and I can touch it all with impunity. I'm invisible.

This close to the border, all the road signs are in English, but we're not in America, at least not the one I grew up in, or the version the rest of the world often thinks of when they consider the Home of the Brave. I think this must be partly why my dad likes it here. Nobody notices him without a second glance. He blends right in. There's no need to explain, no story that needs to be told until the time is just right.

MY FACE IS beige with an olive undertone in the middle of winter, and in summer it deepens to tawny brown, even beneath SPF 50. Nothing can stop it from tanning, as if it's been yearning all winter beneath sweaters and scarves for the sun. I have freckles and moles that neither of my parents have. But when I was a child, I didn't realize I wasn't the same color as my mother until I started playing with her makeup. In her bathroom, she kept bottles and pans labeled *ivory, porcelain,* and *buff,* but when I applied her liquids and powders, they gave me the look of an ashen corpse. Even now, when we go places together, people occasionally ask if I am her "friend," which tells me what they're thinking even if they don't say it aloud: We couldn't possibly be related.

Often enough, when I meet people for the first time, I watch a kind of puzzlement spread across their faces, an algorithm ticking away behind their eyes. Sometimes I understand this look. It's as if we're all hardwired to gauge and to measure, to look upon one another's faces and to file what we see there on whatever racial-ethnic spectrum we've come to observe. But in my case, it's not so easy to guess with a mere glance at the topcoat. I look partially white and partially *something else* in a ratio that changes with the seasons. It shifts with my wardrobe and with the company I share.

But what are you? Where did your family come from before?

I'm not offended by these questions, not really, since mostly they arise from a place of curiosity. But the answer is personal, and so race, to me, has always been an uneasy topic. Sometimes the question comes out of nowhere, without any conversational warm-up. Sometimes people supply guesses without waiting for my reply: Indigenous, Spanish, Mexican, Middle Eastern, or sometimes they just compliment my tan. Is this not like asking someone how much money they make or how they vote? It's not a secret, but could I get a handshake first?

It should be easy enough to say I am half-Indian, as if the other half requires little explanation at all. But I can never really bring myself to do it easily. A series of conundrums awaits. First, I'm obliged to tell a long family history that feels too intimate for an abridged recounting. Who really wants to stand around at the cocktail party listening to the whole saga? I also know, even if the questioner doesn't, that we're headed into murky waters. It's impossible to ask about another's ethnicity without revealing the thing that caught your eye. It's hard to remark that someone is brown, which is to say not-white, and therefore divergent from the norm, without saying a little something about yourself as well. By

then, I am joined inside my foggy cloud of awkward expo-
sure, which is something no one really wants from a casual
bout of small talk. For my part, I try not to ask about anyone's ethnicity, even if I'm curious, even if I sometimes forget. It's none of my business until the information is offered,
and even then, it's still not mine.

What does it mean to be brown? And where does this
racial compartment cleave to whiteness? Sometimes I am
told by friends and strangers alike: "But I don't think of you
as a brown person," which leads to fruit metaphors for the
mismatch of skin tone and cultural fidelity: coconuts, ba-
nanas, etc. I don't speak Punjabi. I have a lot of cousins, and
some of them don't speak Punjabi, either. They don't have
singsong accents or delightful head wobbles or any other
mango-infused idiosyncrasies often attributed to Indians.
But still I wonder in return: Why must it be up to you what
I am? Who gets to decide if not the person wearing the skin?

When you are of mixed race, identity is often contextu-
ally decided, either contested or confirmed by others, as
demonstrated in the case of Barack Obama, the world's
most famous biracial man. In 2010 Obama identified as African American on his census form, though he had the choice
to indicate more than one response. Just a year before, according to a Pew Research Center survey, the perception of
Obama's racial identity varied widely among Americans depending on their own ethnic affiliations. Most white respondents claimed the president was multiracial, whereas most
African American respondents said he was Black. Among
Hispanics, 61 percent said Obama was mixed. Fast-forward
over the next presidency, and conservative Americans were
more likely than liberals to see Vice President Kamala Har-
ris as white even though she doesn't identify as Caucasian at

all; she's biracially Black and South Asian. Perception is
fluid.

Halfsie, mixie, mongrel, mutt. If I'm among light-skinned
people, I'm closer to white than brown. If I'm in India, I'm
same-same but different—brown but westernized. With my
family, I'm just my father's daughter. It's less about skin
than blood. Still, it's illuminating to be almost brown, or
somewhat white, or just ambiguous enough that people let
it all hang out; they feel completely free to be themselves.
Whenever I hear someone begin a sentence with "I'm not
racist, but . . ." I wish I could say I'm surprised. If I had a
dollar for every time I've heard someone drop the words
"towelhead" or "Paki," or gripe about the curry smells, or
bitch about the bhangra in the taxi, or express the open wish
that immigrants just go back to their shithole countries, I'd
be rich.

One of my racial affiliations is "South Asian," a pan-
subcontinental catchall given that India and its neighboring
nations are relatively modern inventions. "South Asian" is a
category that fits nearly two billion people of varying ethnicities who speak dozens of languages and practice many
religions. Nevertheless, my diasporic group is often economically advantaged, with the benefits of family support and
high postsecondary education rates, illustrated by the class
of 2026 at Harvard, which is 27.9 percent "Asian American,"
an even larger ethnic conglomeration, the largest racialized
group on campus.

Skin is an outward-facing phenomenon—an attribute as
unconsciously familiar as the moles on the back of my arm.
Yet it's a prominent, defining feature from without. I don't
think about skin until it's brought to my attention, but some
people never get the chance to forget. I might be half-brown

but I'm also middle-class, straight, cis, very literally a settler, an assimilated one at that. I've never been incarcerated or shot at by the police. Never been put on a no-fly list. Never been the victim of a violent hate crime. Never been told to go back to where I came from—not to my face, not yet anyway. I've never been hungry, never been trafficked or stripped from my family or any of the innumerable onslaughts suffered by racialized people every day. I've been nothing but lucky. My luck has been obscene. So when writers and activists suggest white-passing people step back from their spaces of discourse, I hear it.

I'm half-white. A little milk poured into the tea. Much of the time, like everyone else, I struggle to wear that label. I struggle to understand white privilege, to carry my fair share of a weight that feels like nothing and everything, a phenomenon that divides and multiplies into endless questions. Where does whiteness come from? Who invented it? Is it an experience or a thing that can be owned and worn? I understand whiteness as it occurs in my body, because sometimes I live it and sometimes I don't, depending on where I am and who is looking at me. One state of being illuminates the other.

Whiteness means no harm. It's all apologies. It's just living its best life. It asks what all this fuss is about. Whiteness is found in the hospitality suite, in the premium lounge. It enjoys the freedom to pass through the turnstiles without too much bother at all. Whiteness owns the formula, the secret sauce. Whiteness is a tastemaker. It sips its drink at the party while the staff put out the fires in the kitchen. It gives out the scholarships and then collects the rent. It blesses the food. It says whatever it wants. Whiteness is reason unaffected by desire; it's the instrument of justice. It works hard for the money. It's used to its own reflection. That's all there is. Everything else is a sideshow. It wants to know what your father does for a crust and where you spend your summers. It corrects your pronunciation. But who could turn it down? Whiteness is excellence, it's money, the crème de la crème. It's irresistible, like a shot of junk right to the back of the brain. I know because it runs through my veins.

To me, the most fascinating thing about whiteness is the way it disappears itself, erasing its own tracks. Its roots are a fantastical heritage. Its future is magical also. It notices everyone's complexion, while forgetting to mention its own. It's practically see-through. But to point it out, to speak its name, veers dangerously close to insult.

But what are you really?

Who can tell just by looking?

BORDERLANDS

A DAY WITH THE OLD MAN USUALLY BEGINS WITH ME alone. I often spend the entire morning in the quiet of his dining room, laptop open, burning through a slate of writerly tasks before my dad wakes up and the spontaneities of our afternoon kick in. Then we spend a lot of time just hanging out, enjoying the languid pace of his senior citizenship. To offset the torpor, I make myself squeeze in a little exercise.

I've taken up jogging in middle age—a cliché, I'm well aware. My dad observes this habit with a bemused side-eye, as if I've joined the white Sikhs of Kundalini yoga with their borrowed turbans and kirtan chanting. For my dad, there's no working out, only working. When I'm at his house in McAllen, I run on the down-low, heading out first thing in the morning before he's awake, before the heat of South Texas spreads like a fevered breath across the city. I run to offset my writerly torpor, but also for the psychological maintenance; a good burn lets me outpace my anxieties, at least for a little while, any notion at all that might furrow my brow. And the more he disapproves of any activity, the more I want to do exactly that thing. It's just the way it is. My contrariness is inherited.

Out in the neighborhood the early sky is a wide, uncompromised blue—nothing like the shy pastel of home. My dad lives in a grid of townhomes with brick facades and courtyards ruled by chihuahuas who bare their snaggleteeth through the ironwork when I trot by. The gardens are bursting with hot-weather specimens, Mexican mock orange bushes, hibiscus, grapefruit trees. The air is filled with the upward caws of grackles. Even the turf in my dad's little patch of yard is exotic to my eyes, a jungle carpet of mixed plant life—tough, extremophile turf, not the tender fescues of home.

The Rio Grande Valley would be easy jogging if it weren't for the heat. It's flat as a cornfield. When the wind blows from the south, it's a Mexican style of hot. McAllen belonged to that country for a time, as did much of Texas. Mexico became independent in 1821, and in the ensuing decades, the border was redrawn again and again. Spanish Texas became Mexican Texas, the Republic of Texas, and eventually the state of Texas, not including smaller insurrections like the Republic of the Rio Grande, which is also part of regional lore, with its repeating themes of secession and hard-fought sovereignty.

Beyond my dad's subdivision, the streets are broad and mostly well-kept, lined with palm trees whose dead fronds are pruned by landscaping crews in battered pickup trucks. I run the sidewalks if they are available. Most people drive to get around, but occasionally I see walkers, their dogs panting violently, tongues hanging sideways. Or other runners, whose kindred suffering I acknowledge with a wave.

This place was once an Eden of orange groves, as I'm told by longtime locals. Now it's a bustling little city with shopping plazas, new hospitals, blond concrete low-rises, luxury car dealerships, and high-end jewelry retailers. Before the citrus farms, it was cattle country. And before all of that, this was home to Coahuiltecan peoples, diverse groups with different languages and territories, who hunted and gathered all along the coastal plains. After the arrival of the Spanish, these tribes succumbed to measles and smallpox, or they were captured into slavery or displaced by other tribes. Their movements were poorly understood by European settlers, who lacked the distinctions to identify discrete languages and ethnic groups, or to record family names, once derived from local flora, fauna, and geographical features. Under colonial pressures, these Indigenous groups scattered out to Spanish missions, or they blended into the Hispanic population, their descendants still living here today. Many are still fighting for federal recognition.

The city of McAllen, despite its prevailing Latin influence, is named after an Irish guy whose family ranch, once so large it enveloped the present-day municipality entirely, was part of an eighteenth-century land grant from the Spanish crown. Tejano ranching drove the post-Columbian economy, but with the advent of irrigation and the railway, the money shifted to the commercial farming of citrus, cotton, and sugarcane, industries dominated by Anglo-American immigrants. The collapse of Tejano ranching and subsequent land transfer from Hispanics to whites led to a lot of hardship for many of Mexican American heritage; they faced segregation in the schools, hospitals, and real estate market well into the twentieth century.

Wherever my dad goes, it seems, there is colonialism, dragging its long tail around the corners. After the market crash in 2008, McAllen was a subprime hub infamous for its high unemployment and poverty rates. Yet the city dodged the rampant foreclosures experienced elsewhere, largely due to the brow sweat of its residents, who dug themselves out one mortgage at a time from the predatory lending that caused the whole mess in the first place. These days McAllen has affordable real estate, a booming economy, and a low crime rate—at least according to the city marketing. Yet this town looks somewhat militarized to my peacenik eyes, with its mobile surveillance sky towers and circling helicopters at night. The extra law enforcement shouldn't surprise me, given the ongoing cartel war in the Mexican state of Tamaulipas, which lies just about eight miles away on the other side of the Rio Grande.

McAllen is also famous for its Customs and Border Protection facilities, which house border-crossers and migrants, illegals or refugees depending on your point of view, many from Central America, to whom these centers are known as perreras, dog pounds. During the Trump presidency, the community, and indeed the entire country, faced the specter of children in cages and forced family separations, an anathema with years-long consequences that continued until COVID, when the big CBP building on Ursula Avenue was shuttered, all its detainees sent back across the border. People are still sensitive about this, my dad included—the prospect of freedom and its opposite, living so close together.

. . .

MINE IS A family of immigrants, patched together from motley materials. Today, each of us lives in a different city, as if spread like windborne seeds. I live on the west coast of Canada. My brother is an American citizen who works for Homeland Security—a bit of an irony considering he moves all the time. Our younger sister lives in the UK. This dispersal may have hastened because of divorce, but truly it began much earlier, in my grandfather's generation. As a family, it seems we love suitcases, hotels, and airport lounges, movement and starting over. Sometimes I think we'd go anywhere, without a speck of homesickness or loyalty, if the conditions were just right.

My mother lives in eastern Ontario. In recent years, she's been flying here and there in the company of her husband or her sister, both fellow retirees. On home turf, she's often on the road in her camper van. When we FaceTime, she reveals all her methods for smuggling boxed wine onto cruise ships, or her many crafty ways to go glamping for free. It's sometimes difficult to keep track of her movements. I text my brother when her home phone goes unanswered for a tad too long: *Where's Mama?* I receive her photos and blog-style emails and postcards from Málaga, Portugal, Rome, her many ports of call. In her golden years, she's been having a blast, making up for lost fun. At least for now.

When I'm at my dad's house, he drops hints that I should call her, and I sense he'd love to eavesdrop, or even get a word in, too. He spends a good deal of time rummaging around in memory these days. If only everyone had his talent for releasing the past, if only he could remember how it all blew up in the first place.

Sometimes when I am out and about in McAllen, I consider how weirdly random it is that my dad arrived in Texas at all, as if pinballed here by some fluke of fortune that no one could have anticipated when he was just a boy in short pants, his hair top-knotted, like any good Sikh boy. Now he lives in a town without a gurdwara or a jar of mango pickle anywhere close by, where his friends mispronounce his first name, and he lets them do it with a joyful permissiveness that's new to me, that I seldom experienced in all my childhood.

McAllen's too hot for my northern constitution, but my dad loves it here. He says he has experienced no place in America that's been more tolerant, or easier to make a go of it, without the setbacks of his former lives. It feels to me like a town with a lot of overlap, a place with no single story, which affords a little breathing room for people like him. That's why he'll never move again.

But can you ever truly live in a place, or understand its people, without peeling back the layers of history?

ON THE WAY back to his house, I run across the bridge and stop to look down on the expressway, several lanes of roaring traffic that head northwest along the Rio Grande to Laredo and east to the Atlantic Ocean. Sometimes the reality snaps back to me that I'm *here,* sharing time and space with my dad. I think he's hilarious to be around, very fun generally, with his ageless sense of amusement at life's offerings. We share plenty of preferences, right down to the pizza we always order. This, too, feels uncanny, especially since we didn't exchange a word through all of my twenties and half of my thirties.

When I was just a teenage girl living beneath his rules, there were few areas of my sentient existence that he approved of and vice versa, no expectation of his that I intended to fulfill, because of course I was formed from his minerals, and he's not the docile type. It kind of blows my mind that we've come so far in just a handful of years, transiting around to the opposite of how we used to be. Once I said I'd rather be struck by lightning than let my dad back into my life. But then the decades came to pass, scraping their way over both of us, knocking down the rough edges before melting away, leaving just a few ponds of malcontent in the wake.

Around my thirtieth birthday, the ice was still intact, but my resolve had begun to soften. My grandfather had passed on, rendering the old patrilineal conflict obsolete. The firewall in the family network disintegrated, possibly without a single apology uttered. I'd heard that, with his father out of the picture, my dad had been traveling over to London to visit his sisters for the first time in decades, sometimes in the company of my brother, who was too practical to hold a torch for old miseries. I realized how sad and futile it was that the stubbornness of two men could shape their descendants' destinies, or that one of them had to die for the holes in the bridge to be patched, all those years wasted in the interim. I harbored my own grudge, and I'd squandered plenty of opportunities myself.

Disownment may have worked in the era of steamships and snail mail, but it was harder to maintain in a time of Facebook and daily intercontinental flights. I'd met several of my long-lost paternal cousins on my travels to England, or theirs to North America. They had not the slightest interest in vintage conflicts. We were all my grandfather's Westernized descendants, now with grown-up lives and jobs and some with kids of their own. Our childhoods were so distant and yet so similar. They, too, had been born between worlds and developed expert workarounds when it came to diehard parental customs. It felt odd to have them in my life—and yet not the very person who'd provided our genetic link. My dad was my connection, whether I liked or not, to a pool that was so much larger than just me, all alone.

I was deep into my thirties, the age he'd been when he'd married my mother. By that time, I'd discovered just how much work it was, the project of avoidance, in a big family with an ancestral attachment to ritual, especially if you wanted to attend any of the good stuff, the reunions and celebrations with the sibs, the rellies, the aunties, and the uncles. My dad had faced the same grudge-match trade-off himself—that is, until his parents passed away, thereby disappearing the problem but also his chances of ever really knowing them again.

My reunion with my dad, as it finally came to pass, transpired not out of any distinct plan, but rather, accidentally on purpose. Our paths crossed where such things often take place, at a wedding, my brother's, in Bogotá, far from any mutual turf. From the day the invitation landed in my inbox, I knew it would be mere weeks before I'd have to see my father again, a prospect that filled me with an opposite combo of feelings, relief that an old grievance was ending, but also apprehension. I'd always felt powerless whenever he'd entered a room.

I arrived in Colombia just in time for one of those impromptu gatherings that happens before many a destination wedding, when everyone is jet-lagged and wide awake at odd hours with time to waste and a lot of gossip to catch up on. Everyone knew the granular details of our family saga. All my aunts and uncles and cousins knew precisely who wasn't talking to whom, plus all the backstory. It mortified me still that my offshoot branch of the clan—mom and dad, plus three kids—could be so distinctively nonoperational. This was precisely the failed intercultural outcome that my paternal grandfather had predicted all along. Our family fate also aligned with all the quips I'd ever heard about the perils of mixing blood, as if it was just that simple, the stirring of immiscible fluids, rather than a messy, complicated tangle of love and loyalty, resentments and recriminations, promises made but never kept. I couldn't find the words to explain our dysfunction, nor how we could leave it hanging for so long, and possibly everyone else also found this a little painful, this deep, multigenerational rift, since few in my extended family ever spoke to me about it directly.

A gang of my cousins got together at one of the hotel lounges, and as numerous as they are on my dad's side of the family, they took over an entire corner of the premises with their clustered tables and chairs. And my father, with his nose for party mischief on any continent, snugged himself in among them even though his generational tier of the clan was upstairs in their rooms ironing shirts and shining shoes. That's when I showed up, and for a moment the chatter seemed to hang in the air as everyone's gaze passed from my face to my father's and then back again.

My eye fell upon my dad, who with his supersized personality had always lived as a giant in my memory. Now that we were in person I was surprised by his senior-citizen hair and general bodily mileage, as if the decades had shrunk him down. Maybe I also looked diminished, weathered, tired from the long flight, a little blue at the undereye due to Bogotá's nosebleed elevation, especially when experienced by a lowlander like me. He was wearing a velvet blazer and a shiny maroon shirt, his usual uniform for prowling around on the town. He was the most overdressed person at the table. He wore the same smile he's always had when deep in his element, which is to say in the thick froth of a social function.

A vacant chair materialized next to him, so I sat down. I felt terribly nervous, but my dad turned on the lighthouse of personality and charm. He poured me a politely tiny glass of wine, which I didn't really want, but I threw it back anyway for courage. Then he asked me a question, nothing to do with anything, something casual he might have tossed out to anyone who'd happened to choose a seat beside him, some-one he was pleased to meet for the very first time. It was the way he'd speak to a friend who'd returned from a quick phone call outside. He began as if resuming right where we'd left off, as if no time at all had passed between us, and all was forgiven, if not exactly forgotten.

Another decade has tumbled by since that day, but we don't analyze it. We don't air our former troubles, or even breathe a word about them, just to be safe, in case we back-slide and ruin the good times that remain.

FIBRILLATIONS

IN THE AFTERNOON, MY DAD GETS RESTLESS. HE SUG-gests we go out.

"Want to hit Quinta Mazatlan?" I say, meaning the bird and native plant sanctuary that's just a short drive away. Or really any of the city's delights that confound my preconceptions of what it means to live in the deep south of a red state. The National Butterfly Center? The do-over Walmart library? Or perhaps he wants to assist me in my ongoing search for McAllen's perfect taco? My dad scoffs at all my ideas with his masterfully snaky charm.

Instead, he flips me the keys, and we head out through the back door to the garage, where the washing machine lives alongside his car, empty cigar boxes, some spare flooring, and an old toilet.

Riding around with my dad is an amiable experience. He lets me take it all in without any tour guidance, my edification being long past his concern. It's the opposite of my mother's way, which is to point out every detail in the name of experiential sharing. Many of the local radio stations play ranchera, but that's not my dad's jam. We listen to National Public Radio, which might be the most left-wing thing he does. He chooses for us the scenic route down attractive residential avenues named after war heroes, subtropical trees, other cities south of the Mason-Dixon line.

Occasionally someone will slide through a red light with a cell phone pressed to their face. "Bloody idiot," my dad will proclaim from the passenger's seat, as if this casual impertinence was a personal slight or an affront to the whole of human civilization. "Harvard graduate," he'll mutter at the offending vehicle while shaking his head.

"Harvard graduate" is my dad's cardinal diss. He reserves it for Darwin Award situations, or those moments when people indulge in stupid or trashy behavior, in his opinion. But despite the sarcasm, higher learning is a really big deal—the biggest deal there is. For my dad, a good education is part of what it means to be a good person. You can't have one without the other.

On our trip around town, invariably we end up at his medical clinic, a slightly derelict commercial building near the main street. It's a throwback structure, a faux mid-century modern design with a bit of Spanish-colonial flourish thrown in, next to a large parking lot surrounded by chain-link fencing with weeds growing up from the cracks. Years ago, at a point when most doctors trade their stethoscopes for golf clubs, he gave up surgery to open his own healthcare business. In the heyday, he advertised his services with a carpet-bomb marketing strategy, offering a vast menu of medical services devoted to the rehab of orthopedic issues, pain, work-related injuries, sports injuries, and, according to his website, "any other type of injury." His logo is Da Vinci's Vitruvian Man, penis airbrushed out, and the name on the sign is an acronym that makes perfect sense to my dad if no one else.

At the apex of this venture, he had more than a dozen people working for him, but now in this reluctant phase of semi-retirement, he's down to one, Frances, his office manager, who sits behind the reception glass and gets up to greet us when we walk in. She is a small and gentle woman, born and raised in McAllen, whose ancestors have probably lived around here since the beginning of civilization in these parts. She knows my dad better than anyone, all his tics and foibles. She calls him Dr. Gill, never by his first name, even though she has worked for him for over twenty years. He's fired her several times, or at least he's tried to in his more impatient moments. But still he calls her at least a few times every day, even when he's on vacation, often just to chat. Later on, when it's time to go, she'll load me up with company swag, tote bags and T-shirts and coffee mugs, all emblazoned with my dad's name and many-lettered credentials, even though my collection is full to bursting already.

"Francesca," he says, his tone suggesting he's about to get on her case for something she's done or forgotten to do, even though it's mainly just bluster, a show for my benefit or hers, who knows? "Did you call those people?"

The waiting room is empty of all but a half-dozen chairs and a few fake plants. Yet the aircon is pumping hard, the way he and Frances like it, wafting from the ceiling like a polar vortex. We head into the back with Frances in the lead, her sneakers flashing along the floor, down a darkened corridor. She turns the lights on as we go. The clinic is clean

enough, but with its vintage floor tiles and brown wall paneling, it looks like a mob accountant's office from a seventies
movie. We pass by vacant treatment rooms, then a storage
room perilously stacked with cardboard file boxes and obsolete therapy equipment. Eventually we arrive at the nerve
center of my dad's HQ, his office, a room that highlights
once again his fondness for dark wooden furniture and
brash fluorescent lighting. His big desk sits opposite two
consulting chairs and a bookcase filled with reference
guides—*Current Problems in Surgery, Medical Proof of
Whiplash,* etc. There are also framed photos of his three
kids, quite a few from the awkward, braces-wearing phases
of our childhoods. Being his offspring, we look a tad puffy
about the eyes—a little sleepy, a little sad.

There's also a leather sofa, where I lie down and stare at
the drop-tiled ceiling, wondering if it's made of asbestos,
while listening to Dad and Frances discuss the pressing business, what there is of it these days. This style of waiting is
nothing new. All through my childhood I hung out at nurses'
stations and in doctors' lounges waiting for one or both of
my parents to finish work, drinking orange juice with
chipped ice out of Styrofoam cups. For many people, hospitals reek of clinical hostility, but not for me. The intercom
tones, the beeping monitors, the purposeful calm of nurses
gliding up and down the corridors, even the disinfectant
smells are nostalgic to me. A preparation of sorts for the
inevitabilities of the future, because recently my dad landed
in the hospital himself.

Several years ago, before my trips to Texas truly began in
earnest, I got an email in all-caps from Frances followed by
several urgent texts. My dad had been admitted, she said,
after suffering some kind of cardiac malfunction. In the

weeks before, I'd detected no sign of trouble, except just a trace on the phone. He'd sounded croaky but blamed it on nature. They'd been burning the bloody sugarcane again, he said, in the fields just outside town.

In reality he'd been unwell for weeks but had kept it a secret, like many a senior parent is liable to do, not wanting to add to anyone's worry. There's also the mortal terror of becoming a burden, of being put out to pasture in one's eva-nescent state to contend with the midnight wolves. It could be the most elemental fear there is, one that comes for us all. My dad hadn't wanted to call an ambulance. Instead, Frances said she'd pushed him into the emergency room in a wheelchair, a visual that pained me in the heart. He'd been so big in my life, so unstoppable.

Not long after Frances's email, my phone lit up with calls and texts from family, from people who know and love my dad, from relatives all over the world. My aunt and my uncle, who is a physician himself, were the first to arrive bedside. I should come *right now,* they said, without delay. The next day I found myself in the air, the in-flight wifi down, as if in sympathy. For several hours I didn't know what was happening on the ground. I dreaded touchdown, worried some terrible information was headed my way, suspended in the cloud, waiting to take shape.

I found him in a private room, attended by my aunt, uncle, and brother, who'd also just arrived. My dad was out cold, tucked under a blanket right up to the chin. Beneath that, he wore a voluminous hospital gown—an unthinkable garment, a high fashion crime, he'd probably say, had he not spent a lifetime working in healthcare. He was hooked up to an IV and tethered by many wires to an array of med-ical devices that bleeped intermittently. He'd been out of it for a few days and was barely semiconscious by the time I showed up. He was fine, stabilized, feeling no pain, but nobody yet knew the full story of his diagnoses.

The nurses came and went. Then the cardiac specialists, the hematologist, the infectious diseases specialist, and the respiratory therapists while my dad was pumped full of therapeutic vapors, fluids, and drips, jabbed with finger sticks and blood draws. While he was out for the count, we wondered what had caused this cascade of health issues beyond the obvious fact of his being eighty-something with impeccable resistance to healthy lifestyle practices. Also, why hadn't he gone to the hospital sooner? We continued in this vein of answering our own questions. We agreed that doctors make the worst patients, possibly because they know exactly what they're in for once wheeled through the hospital doors.

We were soon joined in our little family cluster by Frances, who was tearfully relieved to have others share in her burdens. My dad's housekeeper came by to keep Frances company; over their years of service, they'd become friends. We squeezed in together, and with each additional body, we moved over to make more room. This space, with the bed as its defining feature, was comfortable but crowded, with a couple of very upright chairs in the corner. Then my cousin, a radiologist, showed up. Other cousins texted; many of them are doctors, too. And with that, we achieved a greater density of physicians within the room than at the hospital itself, with everyone cross-talking about my dad's labs, his EKGs, his medical history. And that's when the patient woke up.

My dad is living proof that you can make a party of near-death. He returned from his trip to the mortal verge as if to a surprise welcome-home with all of us as his guests. He was back, groggy but wearing a gigantic smile, elated to see us all gathered around him. In the days that followed, more people came to see him, singly or in groups, lawyers in cowboy boots, well-dressed ladies with containers of soup, friends and colleagues and neighbors, until there was nowhere to stand or sit or hear any one conversational thread amid all the loud chatter. If there were visiting hours, I never heard about them. No one kicked us out or asked that we thin the herd, not even the nurses who had to put up with our traffic in their halls.

My dad enjoyed himself immensely, or as much as one can when stationed horizontally in an institutional bed. He never ran out of company. If he pulled the cover from his daily plate and discovered an unrecognizable patty or a small hill of wrinkled peas, he could dispatch one of us to do his gustatory bidding. If he forgot his cell phone passcode for the fortieth time, one of us could wait on hold at Apple. Until our ruckus became too much for him to bear. We were louder than the soft-spoken doctor who attempted to fill him in on the prognosis. Everyone was talking all at once, and he couldn't hear himself think. He couldn't hear the TV. He frowned and grumbled, then issued his signature wave of dismissal, our cue to get out until further notice.

Grumpy. Testy. Bloody well! I knew he was feeling better.

It's still incredible to me that he bounced back in just a few months to his regular state of affairs. Not long after his discharge from the hospital, he was back at home, sleeping in his own bed, dining at all his usual places, smoking cigars, bingeing on late-night Netflix, talking about all the people and places he still had to see in the world, despite making no changes to his diet or lifestyle habits or his shaky adherence to doctor's orders. It must be a credit to his genes or freak luck or maybe a little of both. These days, when we talk about the future or the shape of his mortal adventure, he refuses to take any of it lying down. He won't use his cane or give up his driver's license without a fight. It's clear he intends to do exactly as he pleases—an admirable plan, all told. But from the moment of his first health crash, I could see we were entering a new country where neither of us had ever traveled, but where everyone needs accompaniment.

Now here we are, back at his place of business. Sometimes he puts on his lab coat, the one with the company logo stitched to the lapel, even though there's a for-sale sign affixed to the building outside. In many ways, his career is already over, even if it's hard to swallow. He loves—has always loved—being a doctor. It's a raison d'être, his calling card in the world. To retire is to fossilize, to submit to the entropic tendencies of the universe. And so here, still, is the leather couch in the corner and the school photos in the bookcase. Here is Frances. Here he is behind his desk with the bygone blotter, the paperweight like a little dinosaur egg, his letter knife at the ready.

A WELL-WORN GROOVE

IF WE DON'T MAKE STOPS AT THE STRIP-MALL CIGAR
lounge or the strip-mall Euro pastry shop, by late afternoon we usually end up back in his living room for teatime.
We watch CNN turned all the way up while he commen-
tates on the state of the world. He sits on the sofa. I lie on
the love seat—the usual formation, the ceiling fan lazily
turning above us. The 2020 presidential election campaign
pumps full blast alongside the first impeachment of Donald
J. Trump. It's the last time I'll see my dad before the start of
a global pandemic, but who could guess that this might be
our future?

On-screen, I catch a glimpse of Chuck Schumer, the liberal American senator, with his reading glasses riding low on
his nose. "What do you think of him?" I ask, knowing pretty
well what my dad's going to say, but I want to hear it anyway for my own entertainment.

"Idiot guy," he mutters. He'd change the channel, but he's trying to cram a new set of batteries into the remote control.

I think back to the days when my dad and I watched Tom Brokaw and Dan Rather together, when he changed the channel with a clicker hardwired to the TV with a long brown cable that stretched across the living room carpet, a tripping hazard for all involved. Broadcast journalism has transformed so much since then, but my dad just shrugs it off.

He was born before India's Partition, and in the early parts of his life there was no TV at all. Later, his news came via broadsheet papers. And yet he's adopted the internet with no trouble at all. He books his own flights, with preferences for specific seat rows and even aircraft types, without the assistance of a travel agent. He calls me on FaceTime. He buys nutritional supplements online. During idle moments, I sometimes catch him thumbing around on his phone like a much younger person, leaving a trail of fifty Safari windows open as he surfs.

We talk about the digital revolution and all the people who've lost their jobs and businesses, whole industries on their way down the tubes. The Blockbusters, the RadioShacks, the Yellow Pages, the taxi drivers, the bank tellers. We discuss the way our times have produced a whole generation of well-educated young people for whom there is little room in the economy but for precarity and gig work. There are few guarantees anymore.

All this radical transformation hasn't budged his ideas about stability one iota. In fact, it's only reinforced his conviction that true, watertight security can be found in a limited range of places. To an immigrant, a new land is a jungle of unknowns, and it can take years to trust the game board with all its snakes and ladders. My father has always believed in the tangible world, in things with hard physical form over paper gains or intellectual property. The stock market is like gambling, he says. Real estate over equities, always. If you can't see an asset, touch it, or feel it beneath your feet, then it's probably too risky to own. It can slip through your fingers. It can be torn from your grasp.

On the other hand, work can be counted on without fail. My dad's place in the medical profession has been central to his whole life, fundamental. I wonder aloud, if he's worried about the old retirement stockpile, couldn't he do a few cosmetic procedures on the side?

He looks at me like I've suggested he try dealing oxy or trafficking in human kidneys.

"What about Botox?" I say, knowing full well the disgust this is likely to engender. "A little squirt here and there. Can't you make good money doing that?"

"No," he insists. "I want to be useful."

Only certain professions are right and proper, good for all humankind. My dad abides by what I might call the classic model-minority hierarchy of acceptable trades, in order of prestige: medicine and its variants, including dentistry, pharmacy, and, on a generous day, maybe even veterinary science. Then engineering, followed by accounting and the MBA, but not for nonprofits and only if a six-figure paycheck is involved. Lawyering is kosher, but only as a necessary scourge in a litigious world. The ideal is universal occupational currency, job security no matter where the winds of fate might deposit you and yours. The endgame, at least in my grandparents' culture, a collectivist one at the core, is not to earn big just for yourself, to fill the mansion with Le Creuset and MacBook Airs, but to lift the people around you, too. It's no shocker that my dad and his siblings, all now living in the West, all with grown children, have raised a small army of healthcare professionals. As my husband says, the family weddings make excellent places to have a heart attack.

Many modern occupations probably make no sense to my dad whatsoever. I mean those next-gen, money-for-nothing pursuits that decades ago would have been unfathomable, that even today fall into a limbo of half-reality for those beyond a certain age: YouTube gurus and TikTok comedians, professional gamers and Peloton coaches, Bitcoin traders, the Kardashians. To my dad, these must be the vocational equivalent of cotton candy, jobs spun from air or attention or vanity that produce nothing solid and fulfill no bedrock human need. Whole portions of capitalism succumb to this Fyre Festival, this brave new order of things. But at least they make money. There's that.

Pink- and blue-collar jobs deserve neither scorn nor praise. He acknowledges that "unskilled" manual labor is an unavoidable reality for many, housekeepers and waitstaff, gardeners and construction workers, etc. These are dirty jobs, and someone has to do them. He remains uncharacteristically neutral on this topic, at least when discussing it with me, because for seventeen years—the better part of our silent phase—I worked in the forest industry as a professional tree-planter. This undisguisably grunty job accompanied me through the long apprenticeship of writing and eventually became the subject of a book I wrote, but I'm pretty sure he hasn't read it.

He has never mowed lawns or mopped floors. "I don't know how to make a bed," he once confessed to me with open glee. Today his home is cared for by a tiny phalanx of workers who come and go, vacuuming and mopping and leaf-blowing the tiny patch of lawn out front. He writes checks for that without a shiver of Anglo guilt about it. My dad doesn't do the dirty stuff. I've never once seen him in any kind of workman's attire or even a pair of jeans. Once your clan has walked out of the wheat fields, why would you ever look back?

These days, I'm a contract university professor who teaches into a webcam and holds office hours via Zoom. Online instruction is an oxymoron to my dad; it makes about as much sense as treating someone's brain tumor with Reiki. He was educated Hogwarts-style in lecture theaters featuring blackboards, chalk dust, and a lot of varnished wood. Universities have changed a lot since then, but it pains him to hear about it. For starters, it's no longer a life-or-death scrum to get in. The university curve has been flattened, and some might call it a gift of accessibility and generational uplift, producing more college grads—and more college debt—than ever before. University, I tell him, isn't immune to the pitfalls of corporatization. But back in his day, a degree was something prized, rarefied. You had to compete hard for entrance, and successful exit was not a foregone conclusion. People flunked out all the time.

Professors are not what they used to be, either. The white-haired sages are mostly a thing of the past, as are the bow ties and the one-way orations from pulpits. He hardly believes me when I say I can't fail any student without first phoning upstairs, or that my hotness could be ranked in chili peppers at RateMyProfessors.com until very recently, when that feature was disabled. He won't hear of it, just as he prickles at my suggestion that people are rich, successful, and well-connected because their parents are rich, success-ful, and well-connected. To him, virtue and industriousness live close together in a pyramid of permeable tiers—ascension is determined not by luck or birthright but by the equalizing metrics of hard work.

According to my dad, a $300,000 philosophy degree is utterly pointless, as are most other humanities at any institu-tion, regardless of fees paid. Social sciences, shaky at best. The arts, forget about it. Fine arts, almost morally objec-tionable. It's math and science that paved his way.

I'm well aware that this STEM fixation is a stereotype, one that filters down to TV shows and movies in which book-smart but socially impotent South Asian nerds appear in lab coats as bit-playing doctors and scientists. But what do you do when the cliché is true, or half-true, at least in my family, which is heavily populated with internists, psychia-trists, radiologists, and pharmacists, all of whom are emo-tionally intelligent, seamlessly assimilated individuals who concern themselves with improving the general health of humanity—as opposed to the things I worry about, such as the perpetuation of softly racist portrayals of brown people in popular culture?

The arts may be a crime of wasted opportunity. But peo-ple like my dad and his father and a million immigrants else-where didn't drag themselves from one continent to the next over mountains of paperwork and tangles of red tape, didn't learn new idioms and new secret social codes, didn't study, didn't moonlight, didn't work their fingerprints smooth just so their children could attend community college, or write ghazals by candlelight, or canvass for Greenpeace in thrift-store rags. He and plenty of other foreign aspirants to a bet-ter life did not pull themselves up by the bootstraps, didn't break the family piggy bank, didn't say goodbye to parents, didn't cut their hair, didn't hide their religion, didn't drive taxis or clean toilets, didn't fight their way to the front of the line just so their kids could eat barbecue off paper plates. No way. They mean business.

And in this business, we are all employees in an enterprise built with bare hands from the ground up. The family is like a small private firm with a board of directors containing just two people—mom and dad. The ultimate product is professional children, doctors and lawyers, affluence, respect, and the rights to well-timed parental bragging. And when those kids come of age, they feed themselves into the whole process again, like a great generational recycling. They work themselves down to nubs for their children to become successful, and the children in turn sacrifice their individualistic fancies so their children can soar higher still. And so on and so on, with everyone in a state of perpetual hock, paying it forward while always glancing back.

But in the end, who is the dream really for?

A little joke: How do you find the Indian wedding?

It's at the house with all the silver Benzes parked out front.

Just like plenty of second-gen kids raised beneath the furrowed brows and wagging fingers of their parents, I didn't follow the plan. I did an arts degree and then flaked off like a forest elf into the mists of the Pacific Northwest, where I misspent a good deal of my twenties, followed by a lot of backpacking, dirt-bagging, and the big double-down, a second degree in fine arts. I'm no longer a manual laborer, which must give my dad some relief, at least out in public when people ask what his children do for a living. But even now I don't really care about flashy money, not his, the

Joneses, or my own—a different kind of privilege, maybe. The whys and hows of my strange meandering career make absolutely no sense to him. How can writing be a job, with no office, no salary, and no time clock? How does it pay the bills? How can one live responsibly in this fantasy sphere, where the only product is consciousness transferred to paper? And to be honest, I often ask myself the same thing.

I suspect one of his greatest letdowns is that I never followed in his professional footsteps. I didn't do what was expected of me—openly, without apologies. But then again, neither did he.

I ask him, what would civilization be without beauty, music, storytelling? How would we exist without George Eliot and Leonard Cohen and Rabindranath Tagore and Banksy? Without Prince and Beyoncé? What about all the movies and TV shows he consumes? Someone has to dream them up, then write, pitch, and produce. Isn't the role of the artist to absorb and reconstitute the world's disparities, even to heal its broken parts?

"It's all too esoteric for me," he says.

MY FATHER IS a political junkie whose channel surfing takes him all over the partisan spectrum, from *Morning Joe* to Fox News to Newsmax, from Rachel Maddow to Tucker Carlson. He also knows Canadian politics well and can name every elected official of Sikh descent. He makes allowances for the brown men of broadcasting, which may be the only reason he watches CNN. He can spare a minute for Sanjay Gupta (fellow surgeon, Indian descent) and Fareed Zakaria (Mumbai-born, actual Harvard graduate), who my dad deems "a smart guy," possibly his highest compliment.

During my childhood, he was a Jimmy Carter fan. He's moved to the right over the years, fulfilling the cliché: socialist at twenty, conservative at forty, etc. I can't pinpoint exactly when this came to pass, mostly because we had no contact for the period of transition. At any rate, his contemporary beliefs are an interesting salad of old and new, at first glance paradoxical, but with their own internal logic when I consider his origins, his countries of residence, plus all the decades he's passed through.

He remembers when politics meant Winston Churchill, and the news was Walter Cronkite. He's had a courtside seat for the slow dismantlement of the Empire, through the granting of independence to India, then Kenya, all the way through to the Commonwealth goodbye in the republic of Barbados. He's seen regimes and revolutions, independence movements and military coups. In his lifetime, fads have come and gone and come again. He's lived through wars and assassinations, presidents and prime ministers, natural disasters, the Civil Rights Movement, the sexual revolution, the digital revolution, the twin towers. He's seen the rise and fall of a thousand tides. But he's still here, puffing on cigars, modern cautions be damned.

Like many Republicans, he mistrusts the interference of government in the affairs of regular people. He dislikes bureaucratic bloat and taxes. He believes in evolution but not in climate change, at least not as an anthropogenic phenomenon whose cause is a foregone conclusion. I can't imagine my dad behind the wheel of a tiny electric car. The sixth mass extinction doesn't give him heart palpitations, as it does for me sometimes. What use is "the nature," or its conservation, if you never go out in it?

He is not bullish on socialized healthcare because it clips the entrepreneurial wings of doctors everywhere. When we sit together in his living room solving the globe's problems, he often asks me about the contemporary realities of Canada's universalized medical system, knowing perfectly well the answers.

"How long does it take to get a knee replacement?"

"Quite a while," I say.

Would he be able to procure the specialty prescription he takes for his arthritis?

"Probably not," I admit.

He points out to me with some satisfaction that Canadian one-percenters jet over the border for their elective procedures rather than suffer the long queues with the rest of the plebs. They pay out of pocket for top specialists and cutting-edge pharmaceuticals, which wouldn't exist for the good of the world without American ingenuity.

"At least in Canada nobody goes bankrupt just because they have skin cancer or a baby," I say.

And yet he often surprises me with his quietly left-leaning views. For an OG Indian man, he seems to have little trouble with anyone's sexual orientation, at least as far as I can tell. Abortion is no one's business but a patient's and their healthcare practitioner's. Self-determination is like breathable air to him. It should be free for everyone—or almost everyone. Likewise, he has no tolerance for zealotry or religious violence, especially here in North America, in spaces hard-won by vintage waves of immigrants, who did it the old-fashioned way, on their own steam, facing the added complications of xenophobia and bigotry, who had no mosques or temples or churches of their very own until they built them for themselves. Perhaps this aversion applies most intensely when it comes to his own native religion. He can't abide the kind of extremism that led to the International Sikh Youth Federation or the bombing of Air India Flight 182. As he's told me more than once, "Damn turbans messed the whole thing up."

On the subject of porous borders, my dad is a Texan in the age of white nationalist memes. Legal good, illegal bad. Without a hard line, the bad hombres are coming to town, the rapists and criminals bringing their drugs, their gangs, their fake families. I know I'm not even entitled to an opinion on these matters. I have heard this over and over, a theme my dad repeats to me as well. You have to live in a place like Texas to truly understand.

But what if, I'm keen to ask, you've got to flee for your life with nothing but a toothbrush and a prayer? Waiting in line only works if you've already got time, safety, money to burn. What if you've been banned on the basis of religion? And what if the cops, the economy, the halls of higher education, the banks, the whole system slants against you? Aren't you due for a little redress?

My dad looks at me like I'm a commie snowflake, brainwashed by my Western upbringing into liberal weakness and strange vegan tendencies. Nevertheless, he acknowledges that some people have it worse, the Black descendants of the transatlantic slave trade and Indigenous peoples, for instance. But beyond this, he's steadfast. The rules are the rules. If you want to come to America, you should knock on the door and wait until it opens rather than sneak beneath the fence.

Never mind that the fence, the Trumpian Wall, looks to

me like a Manhattan real estate developer's monument to a crazed idea, a fever dream conceived without the aid of topographical maps. Or that a country composed of immigrants could complain about illegitimate newcomers while living on the expropriated lands of the original inhabitants. Not to mention the paradox of American success, which promises an abundance that's too scarce to share, that aspires to boundless wealth while abhorring inequality, as if filthy richness came at nobody's expense.

I can't help but note the coincidental alliance between my dad's way of seeing things and that niche Republican brand of social Darwinism. Perhaps the white underdogs of deep Trumplandia are better than the white elites on the left. The liberal disdain for the Walmart hordes must remind my dad of the old days and the two-faced Anglos of Great Britain. At least the angry populists are honest about their aims. In this Venn diagram of overlapping beliefs, a tiny sliver of shared worldview emerges: There are only so many dreams to go around, no matter the kumbaya. If you can't trust the Sleepy Joes or the Crooked Hillarys to hear your pleas or defend your cause, then all you have is yourself and your gods to rely on. And beyond that, it's eat or be eaten alive.

I sometimes wonder how a person born and raised in the Third World, as it used to be called in the language of international subordination, could stand alongside a dog-whistling, diversity-averse president with a Dorito-dust tan, even for a minute; this remains a complete mystery to me. How can one be brown, with a good life in a blue precinct of mostly Hispanic voters, and lean red? I have to remind myself that my dad isn't simple because most humans aren't simple. They are changeable and complex, and just because one has faced prejudice, it does not make them one-dimensional, or any less likely than a white person to possess their contradictions.

This goes in the direction of many of our debates. We're already practically shouting over the TV.

"But, Dad!" I say.

He waves the remote control at me like a scepter. I argue. He argues back. Left. Right. Old. New. Then we reach a crescendo, a point at which we stop on the edge of acrimony, reluctant to take it any further. We've had our share of blustery disagreements, our points of no return. He shakes his head and mutters in my direction. Then he gives the air an emphatic swat, as if to banish me back to my commune of wokies, a place where everyone listens to Bon Iver and drinks kombucha out of mason jars.

Our disagreements are a well-worn groove, not just one that we've carved out for ourselves, but also one Indian fathers and daughters have been having ever since the first desi walked out of his ancestral village in search of milk and honey.

16

BUBBLES

JUST WHEN I THOUGHT WE'VE REACHED THE PINNACLE of our new and improved father-daughter relations— mostly affectionate, spiced with the odd semi-theatrical dustup—we are torn apart once again, but not by a breach of our own making.

At the start of the coronavirus pandemic, my father and I are separated by the cross-border traffic ban, a development my dad condemns as "bloody rubbish." The restaurant shutdowns are also rubbish, a deprivation for him, who in regular circumstances makes daily visits to all his usual haunts. There's takeout, but that is entirely beside the point. Eating out is less about food than human interface, seeing and being seen. What could be lonelier than a Styrofoam container and a lone plastic fork, with no dal makhani anywhere in DoorDash range?

The world has crawled into its shell. Everything is canceled. My dad takes to video-calling me, just like millions of housebound, socially isolating parents and grandparents all over the world who are cut off from tactile contact with their progeny. He prefers to see my face, I suppose, since we're destined to be apart for the murky, unseeable future.

He calls me from the red-bricked courtyard of his neighbor's house, where he has attended at least a few illicit barbecues. At these unsanctioned gatherings, I'm floated around on his phone for the purposes of greeting the hosts and fellow guests—all people I've never met before even though they live just a few steps away from his townhouse. It's a blur of unmasked faces, potted tropical plants, and barbecue smoke, a small crowd of men sitting around a table looking happily beset by postprandial fatigue.

"Aren't you supposed to be staying home right now?"

"Heh, heh," says my dad, "I'm cheating a little bit."

Other times, he calls me from his living room, where he watches the pandemic unfold from the sofa. "I'm so bored," he confesses. Everything is closed, including his business. There's nowhere to go. He reminds me that he's already been stuck in McAllen for a few years now—ever since his last hospital stay, he's found it difficult, health-wise, to travel. Shutdowns are bad for the economy, but it's been brutal for those rendered jobless, on that we can both agree. And with all this enforced solitude and austerity, he says, isn't everyone beginning to suffer emotionally and psychologically?

As a doctor, my dad believes mental health is best addressed in the psychiatrist's office. But like many immigrants, he's not exactly a fan of psychotherapy or talking cures for himself. My dad has never tended to blurt or over-tell, as if to do so invites further calamity. If he's within earshot of gossip, he'll make an ameliorating comment, some dignity-preserving bon mot about the person in question, and then he'll change the topic. Similarly, he has no taste for schadenfreude, except when it comes to my mother's now-husband, a man he calls "Mr. Nick," followed by his signature chuckle. His way of dealing with trauma, if he even believes in such a concept, is to go forward, to walk through the gates with a one-way ticket and then never look back on your troubles.

According to my dad's philosophy, it might just be a Western notion that suffering and happiness are mutually exclusive experiences, that laughter can't live alongside pain. Or that bliss must be total in order for it to exist at all. He's mostly chipper as heck, I could say compartmentally so, even during a viral apocalypse. He wears his optimism like a uniform.

Soon enough, Texas is open for business again almost as quickly as the shutters descended. Dad goes back to his old tricks. He calls me every couple of days to tell me about the business at the clinic and who he had lunch with and who among his so-called friends is in his bad books. His backdrop is often the patio of his preferred café, or the cigar lounge where it's scenically impossible to pretend he doesn't smoke cigars. He won't listen to reason. I can't tell him what to do. He's a somewhat-retired physician with a tobacco fancy in the midst of a global respiratory emergency. With his various medical concerns and pharmaceutical regimes, he's remarkably free and easy with his precautionary measures, even at the healthiest of times. But he's also in his eighties. And maybe, if I get to be his age, I won't care to waste a day on anything but living, either.

The hair salon he's been patronizing for twenty years has

also reopened, ending a period of enforced lockdown bushi-
ness that seemed to irritate him as a matter of hygienic hardship. It pained me to witness his overgrown haircut and five
o'clock shadow, since he's always immaculately groomed,
right down to the fingernails, which he usually has mani-
cured at a nail joint a few minutes from his house. At this
acetone-scented parlor he has his hands buffed and clipped
right alongside Latinas getting ballerina gel nails in cotton-
candy colors.

He turns his head to show me the newly shorn sides, a
return to his old self. "Your dad is losing his hair," he muses,
as if each new bout of aging comes as a slight surprise.

"I think you're doing pretty great," I reply.

"My hairdresser says she doesn't know how to part it
anymore. Maybe I will comb it forward!" Then he laughs,
chuffed by his own improv.

My dad's views on the pandemic are pretty much what I
expect, Republican with a homeopathic drop of disquieting,
scientific truth. He says face coverings don't work. I think
that's funny coming from a man who spent most of his
working hours in operating rooms. "But now they have the
masks with the gold and the designer logos." Despite these
minimizations, he managed to procure two vaccinations before the civilian rollout truly began.

Coronavirus, he tells me, is an infection that mostly be-
falls the elderly. I gently suggest that this is actually *his* demographic, but he waves me away. Of course he knows his
age, intellectually at least, even while claiming exemption
from actuarial statistics, if not mortality itself, which I sense
is a form of magical thinking I'll succumb to myself one
day—and not only because I'm composed of his DNA. Is

this not the hope that allows us all to keep on living in the face of an unknowable beyond?

The world might be stricken with a plague, and yet some days, my dad seems more contrarily vital than ever. He digs out some of his nicer blazers, the double-breasted ones with the flashy buttons that he usually keeps in reserve for medium-upscale occasions. At the other end of the spectrum, I sometimes catch him in the shirts he's owned for decades; one was a gift from my sister way back in the eighties, purchased at JCPenney, now with a disintegrating, frayed collar.

"You're falling apart," I say.

"It's the fashion," he quips. "All the young people are wearing it." The richer the kid, he adds, the more destroyed the clothing. I nod in silence and admire the irony of shredded, made-in-Bangladesh attire, especially as worn by an elderly South Asian male.

He asks me, just as he does every single time, when I'll be able to visit, quarantine orders be damned. He keeps meticulous track of the time elapsed since my last visit, which he announces every time we talk. "Six months," he says.

Before COVID, I saw my dad with semi-annual regularity, but now I worry about him quite a bit, a low-level anxiety that will reach its peak in the second year of the pandemic when a record-breaking storm hits Texas, plunging much of the state into a deep freeze. In a place where people's HVAC concerns are mostly devoted to aircon, over two hundred people will die, most from hypothermia. My weather channel streams video of snow in the palm trees, burst pipes, and indoor icicles, and even without a border closure and a worldwide pandemic, there isn't a thing I can do about it.

My dad survives without any power or heat for a few days, huddled up inside in the dark. He manages to get himself installed in a friend's empty condo on the other side of the town where the electricity has been restored.

Winter gives way to spring, but there's little in the way of renewal. The pandemic is just like a pressure cooker, that's what people say. Millions pour into the streets in support of Black Lives Matter. My dad watches it all unfold from the middle cushion of his sofa. He listens, in his conservative media milieu, to commentators discussing race, bias, and privilege. Sometimes he calls me to keep him company, which I guess is his way of making sense of it all.

For my dad, racism is still a thorny topic. One can be a person of color with extreme privilege. And being brown exempts no one from the pitfalls of prejudicial thinking; it's quite possible to receive the slings and arrows of discrimination while hurling them out yourself.

Just look at India, my dad points out. One need only glance at the uneven distributions of the caste system, which still survives on the subcontinent and in the diaspora, despite the fact that it's illegal to discriminate on this basis. Sikhism may be a casteless faith, and yet anyone in the know can ask me my surname and derive a host of clues about my family history, its religious customs, its ancestral region in the homeland—even though no one but distant relatives have lived there for close to a century—and I can be judged accordingly. There's also the infamous South Asian preference for light skin, especially where women are concerned. Fairness conflates with beauty, virtue, and even upward mobility, as reflected in the everlasting popularity of Unilever's Glow & Lovely, a rebrand of Fair & Lovely, the holy grail of Indian skin-bleaching products in a multibillion-dollar lightening market around the world. Not to mention the phenomenon that had flamed my dad in the first place—the one that made me and the entire shape of our misfit, half-brown family—the taboo against intercultural couplings, however those might look.

I'm also unable to forget my family's time in East Africa, its footprint there, its historical trace. The well-being and security that my grandfather built in Nairobi meant he never had to return to the village. But we owe our good fortune, at least in part, to the imperial favors of an apartheid system. In my grandfather's day, Kenyan Asians, as Indian immigrants like my grandfather were called, endured the downward pressures of the colony, but they also benefited at the expense of local tribes whose land they'd occupied alongside the British. I've never lived anywhere, not the United States or Canada, that hasn't been touched by similar forces, where one population's gains aren't built on the losses of another, or so it seems according to the zero-sum game.

Lately my dad laments that "everything comes down to complexion." It's as if an old, hidden order has been disturbed—a necessary reckoning, but still a hierarchy he's worked his whole life to navigate like a hedge maze with elusory exits. I suspect he liked it better when trouble rippled beneath the surface, when only racialized people cared about this stuff or thought about it daily. Out in the open, it feels dangerous. Maybe he preferred it when prejudice was personal, when it was his issue and no one else's, a private affliction surmountable through head-down toil and a thickened lizard skin. As if, in all his Western years, he'd found proof that industriousness, success, or even shameless ostentation could disguise the obvious fact that he is brown, with an accent, not even close to natural-born. Maybe that's why he doesn't really want to talk about it now. I guess it's a luxury to discuss it openly, to have the emotional and mental resources available at whatever time of day you're feeling it.

When I'm at home, I sit around in socially distanced circles talking with friends about what it means to be an antiracist and an ally. And yet the world seems more stuck in its race cocoons than ever. Much of the time, I struggle to contribute to these chats. As a semi-white person, it's strange to be both-and in a world that's increasingly either-or.

Even when I write it feels impossible to make a single sentence without someplace definitive to stand. Every phrase reveals some leaning one way or another, a bit of personhood or history, some whiff of aversion or longing; every line betrays a worldview. I stare at the blinking cursor, and the question presents all over again. *What are you?* No matter where I hope to go, there's always a little fraud.

IN MY OTHER professional life, I teach writing. My daytime gigs are in academia, where words like "equity" and "inclusion" float around like confetti bomb discharge. In the months before COVID, I spent many hours applying and reapplying for jobs, a process that ends abruptly once all the universities and colleges empty out. Nothing much ever comes of it. In a way, this comes as a relief, since the process involves flights and hotels and panic-inducing campus visits with research presentations and mock-teaching sessions, not to mention awkward dinners that nobody really wants to attend.

At these interviews, without fail, I'm asked to outline my "diversity practices" before selection committees who can't decide if I am BIPOC or not, or if it's even legal to ask. I wade into the swamp of vulgar guesswork, too, since to me these committees appear composed of mostly white people. Not uncommonly, the only brown contingent is the nonvoting student reps or recent hires whose eyes stay glued to the university-endorsed question sheet set before them.

Help me out, I want to say. How do I begin to answer these questions? What teaching strategies will I implement to further the university's mission of equity, inclusion, and decolonization? How will I enact these mandates at every level, from the classroom to the committee table?

Of course I study up in advance, just like thousands of other job hopefuls duking it out in competitive HR environments. I consult online discussion forums and academic blogs for the secret methods of crafting a winning answer. Ideally, diversity can be performed by anyone regardless of race, ability, sexual orientation, or gender identification. But no matter how much incredible stuff I learn, I'm still confused by the prospect of the "diverse" student or applicant or even human being. Collectives can be diverse, workplaces can be diverse, but how can anyone, as an individual, be diverse? Diverse from what exactly, marked against what baseline state of being? And am I meant to be diverse for myself, or do I carry it on behalf of others? If so, who are these others? Are they my students, the queer Métis novelist or the poet in the hijab who never gets airtime in the workshop? Or is it my prospective bosses, the unseen board of governors?

As soon as this question comes out at the big committee interviews, time seems to stop, and the dust particles hang in the air. I'm nervous I'll mess it up, but I also feel the weight of it all. My eyelids want to close. I want to put my head down on the conference room table and drift off into narcoleptic oblivion.

Part of a successful diversity statement, the advice forums recommend, is to openly declare one's own subjective positioning. But I shrink from that task, too. I don't want to state my race. I don't know what it is, not exactly, and not knowing doesn't feel like a brand or a professional asset. It feels like vulnerability, like a crack in my central story, as personal to me as declaring the color of my underwear in the middle of a job talk.

I don't think I want to be known as the diversity hire, or to be told that I've received any accolade or paycheck or stray crumb of goodness just by weaseling past some better-qualified, normal, non-diverse person. I'm not sure I want to be ambiguously ethnic, either—just brown enough to pull it off, but sufficiently white to make a good "fit," with my domesticized accent and bland, interview-appropriate clothes. I don't want to compete with someone browner and more deserving, according to some quantum of melanin whose terms are never explained to me, someone closer to home or more "authentic," however such things are determined behind closed doors. I don't want to be cursed by resented mandates, by the very remediations designed, in theory anyway, to correct historic imbalances—a status quo created by and for non-divergent people whose unexamined non-differentness is seldom the subject of interview questions.

I don't know what diversity is beyond some deeply flawed bullshit. That's what I really want to say. But if that's all there is, do I have to take it? My utility bills don't care about diversity, and neither does the bank who owns my house, which sits quite literally on pilfered land, just like many a university in the Americas, with all their glassy libraries and shiny gyms and state-of-the-art research facilities. How on earth does anyone decolonize without giving any of it back? Wouldn't that be the first place to start, not with me and my little syllabi?

BEIGE UTOPIA

I MIGHT PASS FOR WHITE SOME OF THE TIME, BUT NOT always and definitely not forever. I've never known how to game it. There's no abiding rule with which to win. And even if I do get away with it, what is "it" exactly besides escaping a fate that others can't avoid? It's getting things for free, the active verb seems to imply, that other people have paid for. It's slipping through the gap in the gates. It's complicity. It's cheating. As if the fault lay there, in the disguise. This has never felt easy to talk about, not even with my siblings, in our range of melanized tones.

At birth, my twin and I shared the same skin color. But then we grew into different shades. He's also an amorphous brown, and he could be many things, but with his Indian brow and my grandfather's nose, he's seldom mistaken for a white person. When I see him immersed within the Indian side of the family, amid a gang of our cousins, his provenance is unmistakable. He's undeniably a part of them, whereas I am related but slightly offset, a variation of the visual theme.

Several years ago, we attended a family wedding—on the English side. We took the trip to the United Kingdom with our mother but brought along no plus-ones. This was a Christian wedding in an old stone church on the outskirts of London, our mother's terra firma, complete with the usual mystery rites, the fuzzy stuff of memory we'd absorbed from her as children but had never adopted ourselves. We stood out in a room full of light-skinned people, some of whom had received spray tans for the occasion, Alex and me in our shared half-Indianness in a small sea of our mother's people. The ceremony was followed by a period of mingling in a hotel banquet room while we waited for the reception to begin. It's the kind of affair I find slightly sweaty and uncomfortable, especially among strangers. That's where I came across my brother, who was standing with a cluster of old men in morning suits and tailored wool.

Alex was talking with a short man holding a short drink. My brother had recently gone back to school as a mature student. He'd completed an MBA at an American university whose name the man didn't recognize. "Not exactly Cambridge, is it?" the man said with a dry little laugh.

I barged into the conversation and introduced myself as the sister—a slight impertinence, it seemed. The man nodded and smiled then turned from me back to my brother again. "How nice," he said, "when the colonials get to travel."

Maybe the man meant nothing by it, nothing but a Britishly friendly joke. Maybe it wasn't about ethnicity or foreignness or class, all those vectors that seem to crisscross like an invisible web beneath our interactions. Maybe, but maybe not. That's always the way it is in situations such as these. Usually, I'm left with a terrible case of esprit de l'escalier, still wondering long after the moment has passed and everyone else has forgotten. It feels oddly embarrassing to write such things now, as if the error is mine, the impression all wrong. But I imagine, in an alternative version of the day, that nothing might have been said at all if my brother was white, or even a slightly more deniable shade of brown. If I'd been alone, or with my mother by my side, I might have slid through the room for just a little longer.

Why must it be up to others what I am? In the end, I arrive at a tentative destination, a place of reluctant acceptance. My mixed identity belongs to me, but only partially. The slider moves with the environment, the company I keep, or the mood of strangers at any given moment. Perception is half of the story, if not most of it, whether I approve it or not. My origins are mine to call whatever I want, but if the world, by its glancing assessments, decides I am white or Anglo or whatever to call this soft-bordered designation, then shouldn't I accept the weight? Shouldn't I bear responsibility for passing, even if half of me is erased?

WHAT DOES IT mean to be Indo-Saxon, merged from two distinct, collided lineages, and yet to be something else on the outside—just generically, muddily brown? I'm hardly alone in it. Mixed-race humanity is all around me, seemingly everywhere I look. I meet them in real life, they're my friends, relatives, passersby. But they're even more omnipresent, in greater densities than ever before, on Netflix, the internet, the pages of magazines. They're ubiquitous, these some-other-race people who are a little bit white and a little bit something else—but always a little bit white. They have curls, freckles, amber eyes. They look fit and cute, healthily appealing in their ambiguously global way. They dance and road-trip with their rainbow assortments of pals. Everyone is happy, laughing, stealing one another's french fries, frolicking around in autumn leaves, collaborating thoughtfully at work while wardrobed in the same blandly neutral style, as if in a sunny near future where everyone shops at Gap. Everybody's having a fantastic upper-middle-class time. Nobody's the Uber Eats delivery guy, the security guard, the dude at the car rental place who vacuums our crumbs from the floor mats, the lady at the nail salon who crouches over our calluses. Everyone lives together in harmony without a smidge of lopsidedness, without poverty or prejudice, in an upscale, coffee-colored dream world.

I appreciate this public imagery—in ads, TV shows, and even PSAs—for the way it makes a space, the way it carves out a little more real estate for the growing mixedness of our times. But I love them for the way they reflect reality—the individuals, couples, and families who have always lived among us without a reflection or reference point in the world, their existence unshared and unseen. Marketers might resist inclusive imagery for fear of alienating white consumers, but if research is any indicator, they also run the downside risk of ignoring "other" customers, people who might engage—and open their wallets—if presented with same-race ethnicity cues.

And if mixedness is cool or hot today, there's no way to imagine a world of medium-brown people without the precursors of mixed parents, which can still touch a racist nerve, if online vitriol is a measure, especially when it comes to white people with Black partners in the media. For some in the audience, televised interraciality pushes an idea, a clandestine form of social engineering whose logical extreme is white extinction or the "great replacement," the alt-right belief that immigration and woke multicultural messaging are a part of a conspiracy to obliterate the Caucasian race.

The perceived extinction of American whiteness by a minority supergrowth is a concept incidentally reinforced by the most recent census numbers in the United States. At least it appeared that way, since the white population experienced a drop of nineteen million in one decade, an 8.6 percent reduction. By contrast, the multiracial population jumped by 276 percent. In reality, these renovated stats arose from a change to the census questionnaire itself, an accounting correction that granted expanded options for racial self-expression. Respondents who'd previously qualified as solely white could now reclassify themselves as Latino, multiracial, or mixed-race—what they'd always been to begin with. The white populace isn't really shrinking, it's merely losing some of its market share.

Historically, there is no special category at all for individuals of Middle Eastern or North African descent—according to the Census Bureau, they are white even if they don't identify that way. A similar accounting trend occurred in Canada; on the 2016 census, "Jewish" was offered as a religion but not as a prompt for the ethnicity question, and as a result, half the Jewish population vanished, at least on paper. In Canada, Métis and non-status Indigenous peoples weren't classified as "Indians" by the federal government until 2016, following a lengthy legal fight by the Congress of Aboriginal Peoples for those rights and recognitions. And nobody's ever really known where to put mixed-race people. We're a moving target.

However they are counted, multiracial people might make for one of the fastest-growing demographics in the Western world simply because they are being seen and accepted for the first time outside mutually exclusive race categories. In the United States, 33.8 million people now identify as two or more races, comprising over 10 percent of the American population. In 2011, the United Kingdom counted more than 1.2 million mixed-race Britons in a population of 63.2 million, a total almost doubled from the prior census. Canada doesn't directly enumerate by race, but interracial unions accounted for 4.6 percent of all couples in 2011, a number that nearly doubled in two decades. By recent estimates, mixed couples make up 7 percent of all legal partnerships.

A LOT HAS changed since the days of Everett Stonequist and his marginal, half-caste subjects. But mixed-race people still receive their fair share of sociological curiosity. Multiracial individuals are more attractive, their heightened overall sexiness allegedly due to hybrid vigor—at least according to one study. But biracial folks are also bad for a party, according to another study. They make people socially uncomfortable. Their racially ambiguous faces tax the brain, foiling the old cognitive systems that dictate how we should apply race labels and who we should in-group or out-group.

It's difficult to think about hybridity without sliding backward into race and its auxiliaries—purity, miscegenation, half-bloodedness. These concepts feel as old as the mountains, so entrenched in received beliefs around human diversity and societal organization as to seem self-evident. But aren't we all infinitely hybridized?

My own ancestral stew, according to one of those spit-tube DNA tests, is a mashup of European influences, British and Irish, French and German, combined with my dad's monolithic "Northern Indian & Pakistani" contribution. I share these genetic macros with my siblings. And yet we can have markedly different experiences in the world—even as we share feelings of partial belonging. We can walk up to the front door on either side of the family. We can knock, receive a welcome, and enter, but we can never truly be inside. Instead we have something else, a third thing in want of a better name that's always on the tip of my tongue.

I sometimes imagine another reality, with an alternative set of parents, the ones we might have had but didn't, an imaginary couple formed from aligned racial ingredients, born in a shared world, enmeshed from the start, annealed in history, language, and culture. I think about how it all might have looked if we'd stayed together—if, on my adult visits, I watched my parents sit beside each other at the dining room table or go out together on evening walks. I can't picture what we might have been like if only we'd learned the fine arts of peace, contentment, and compromise. That's not the way it shook out, despite anyone's best intentions. Instead, we've been shaped by the forces of dispersal rather than conglomeration. If I zoom way out, this drift traces back to no one person. Instead of branching and building up, we've dwindled, floated out, stretched the limits of what might still count as "family."

Sometimes I swear I'm nothing like either one of them, but of course that's impossible. I think of all my dad's quirky proclivities. He can't eat a boiled egg, or really any bland food, without labeling it first with Tabasco or Tapatío. We share a love of spicy gingersnaps as well as a hatred for creamy soups and white sauces. But most of all, we dislike being told what to do. We'll run in the opposite direction, right into the arms of the most contrary behavior available, which makes us quite susceptible to reverse psychology.

I think of the way my mother makes tea, in a Brown Betty pot, always with her much-abused cozy. This is the way I make it, too, in this English fashion, once removed from my own experience. I've learned how she sharpens her kitchen knives like samurai swords. Great for a loaf of bread, but if you set them free in the dishwater, you risk losing a finger. My mother sticks her tongue out when she's concentrating hard on a crossword, which she always nails, no matter the degree of difficulty, with a pen in a single sitting. When she goes out to a restaurant, she takes photos of her food as if the plate is a little work of art, worth more in the saving than the tasting. I remember her handwriting scrawled all over everything in our little world, on all her lists and labels. If objects weren't systematized, we might forget their purpose or lose our hold on them forever. I consider her wedding ring, a simple gold band, which she didn't remove for a long time after she and my father separated. She never changed her name, either, not even after her second wedding, as if her commitment to an over-the-top Indian man was not a thing that could be ended so simply, not with a mere divorce, not with her clutch of half-brown kids in the mix.

I still wonder if something might be salvaged from their pioneering intercultural explorations besides three racially ambivalent, culturally betwixt, downwardly mobile offspring who turned out well enough, but perhaps not as bragworthy or productive in the grandkids department as either of them might have liked—since here we are the experiment's conclusion, the end of the family line.

When I think about how to belong or what to call myself, it's difficult to reconcile my parental lineages. I'm just as Indian as I am British at heart, which is to say not much of either. Not authentically, as it's often said here in the West to describe proximity to the source, no matter how diffuse or hybridized those origins were to begin with. And yet I am both those things by association, by blood and allegiance. What does it mean to be almost brown, with an incontrovertibly English mum and a lapsed Sikh for a dad, our shared lives shaped by a past everyone thought they forgot? Maybe it should mean nothing, ideally. Not much more than love and negotiation.

IT'S DOPE TO be mixed-race these days. That's what people tell me. Yet it feels bizarre to be on-trend as a biological personage, as if one day soon my whole being will fall out of fashion and return to its rightful place in the background, as if that's where it belonged all along. My DNA will exhaust its limited possibilities, and life can get back to the way it used to be, just regular and normal.

Pretty soon we'll all be living in a demi-brown utopia. I hear that, too. This might be an idea brushed along by the prevalence of mixed faces and bodies in commercial culture as well as burgeoning multiracial demographics. But I'm just not sure how a mixed-race baby boom could pull off the work of anti-racism efforts that activists and scholars have needed whole lifetimes to achieve, feats of systemic disman-

tlement that no one's truly been able to reach for all the resistance and obstruction, even after centuries of trying.
Interraciality can exist alongside racist structures with perfect intactness, especially if you are Black in America or Indigenous in Canada or identified by ethnicity in any number
of places around the world. And how could mixedness ever
be a revolutionary or world-saving idea when "multiracial"
is so often portrayed as partially white and usually straight,
leaving all kinds of people out in the cold?

I'd like to believe that the future is beige, but I'm also a
little doubtful. It's not like ethno-racial mixing is anything
new. And despite my mixed blessings, as numerous as they
are, I don't think I love the idea of a continuing reality in
which one kind of flesh is superior or luckier or more deserving than all the rest. I want no skin in that game.

INHERITANCE

FINALLY, THE BORDER OPENS AGAIN. I SEE A LITTLE window, and just like my dad has always done, I take my chance and slip through. A nasal swab and three flights later, I'm back in Texas. It's been two years since I've seen my father in person. The time in between has seemed to melt while simultaneously freezing into a solid.

My dad picks me up at the airport, wearing a big smile, looking dapper as ever in biscuit-colored trousers and a shiny black shirt, gold watch hanging loose as a bracelet on his wrist. He's ready to go wherever the night takes us. It's September, but this far south it still feels like summer. The midnight sky has a thickness, the humidity clouding the stars. I toss my suitcase in the trunk of his little red car, which appears to be soldiering on, scuffs, scrapes, and all.

"It's nice to see you," he says.

"You look good," I reply.

He decides to take me out for a very late supper, and we head to his favorite steakhouse. Not coincidentally, the restaurant is walking distance from his place, though he always drives, preferring to roll up in the valet zone even though it isn't a parking spot, and he already has a blue parking permit hanging from his rearview mirror anyway. No one at the restaurant seems too concerned about this; they just let him use it for his own purposes.

His car, like most of his historical vehicles, is an impractical lowrider with no back seat. He exits using a double-leg swing and a quick vertical struggle that no one notices unless they're expressly paying attention. In a few short steps we're inside the courtyard. The staff hail my dad by name as we pass by.

My dad has a favorite alfresco table in this establishment that he's been coming to for years. Upon arrival, I realize that he's been here for quite a while already, and that my airport pickup was merely an interlude to a session in progress. There are two dudes holding down the fort amid a fair bit of tableware clutter. They know my father from the sales end of the medical trade; they come here a lot from Houston on business trips. We arrive into a political discussion that includes some griping about COVID restrictions and President Biden. These guys are new to me, and I can tell from my dad's dampened responses that he never really invited them over. They just sat down, which is standard operating procedure in my dad's little corner of the universe.

After my dad's questionable friends depart, he waves down a waiter and orders pasta. I order chimichurri steak. At home, my crisper drawer sees a lot of action, and my grocery lists rarely implicate any animals. But whenever I'm in Texas, for reasons that elude me, I surrender all my herbivorous tendencies. At my father's favorite restaurant, he sometimes orders for the both of us. Not unusually, it's chateaubriand, which does not appear on the menu, or beef Wellington. When I'm with my dad, it's all about blood on the plate.

Tonight my dad's dish arrives as a starchy tangle in cream sauce. He makes a face before the plate can even touch down on the tablecloth. Then he probes this dish briefly with a fork before sending it back to the kitchen, which has already been wiped down for the night. Then he orders something else that he has little intention of eating, that I will likely finish so it doesn't go to waste.

My dad has mastered the art of dining out without ever really eating at all. He's an excellent conversationalist, always has been; it's one of his diversionary tools. Often we stitch together memories of the houses and cities we've lived in together, the friends with whom he's lost touch. He'll discuss the annals of his medical career, the patients, the bedside vigils, the procedures and pacemakers. Occasionally he drops a deeply incorrect nugget of observational humor, sprinkling in a little Spanish to conceal the most off-color notes. The joke is often followed by an amused chuckle, to show how much he enjoys flaunting the world's newfangled rules, and to show he knows that I know it, too.

Sometimes we don't talk at all. We just sit and watch diners come and go, the extended family groups, the tables of single women celebrating birthdays, the anniversary dates, the business travelers in jackets and white shirts, burning up their per diems. Everyone is accustomed to seeing him here at our table for four. He lights up when someone comes around that he knows, especially if the someone is a woman. If an acquaintance ventures over to say hello, he invites them to join us. He introduces me as "his girl," which elicits looks of startled wonderment, fleeting moments of worry that I might be his terribly age-inappropriate date. Wine is topped up, and lighthearted banter ensues.

My dad is a moth—a nocturnal social butterfly. Maybe the late-night crowd presents more scintillating possibilities, a chance he can catch some action just as it's just starting up in the cantina. He'll fall in with friends, other retired bachelor-professionals, the kind of people who show up at restaurant bars after ten P.M. on a weekday. I can never keep up with my elderly, socialite dad, by whom I'm regularly outpaced and outpartied, who likes to stay up long after my eyelids begin to droop.

"Dining is my only luxury," he says.

This is mostly true. It's the highlight of our time together, but it also hurts me in the heart to think of this lifetime expense, what good it could do elsewhere, what good it might have done years ago for me, my siblings, my mother. But it's his choice, and he always pays. In an extended family of doctors and pharmacists, I'm the sole creative type, the only professional loser. I could never afford to eat this way unless it was on someone else's dime. A free dinner is still a gift to me.

The vegetarian trophy meat. The deliciously wretched excess. All these awkward realities sit side by side, which is the way it's always been between us.

MY DAD AND I resume our usual pattern, spending days like there's no tomorrow—sleeping in, commenting on the news, comparing our strategies for ruling the world.

I set up my laptop at his big glass dining room table. It

becomes my office for working remotely. Whenever he passes through on the way to somewhere else in the house, he stops to see what I'm doing, to advise me of our plans for the day, or just to chat, his hand lingering around the dimmer switch, or on the back of one of the chairs.

"Hey!" he says. "Do you want that?" He points to the giant painting that hangs behind me on the wall.

This artwork reflects my dad's tastes—abstract and visually blaring, but also huge, several feet wide, in a heavy gilt frame. "I like it," I say. "But how would I get it home?"

He shakes his head and flaps his hand at me as if to imply I shouldn't concern myself with such minor logistical trifles. Next, he asks about his furniture, referring to his massive dresser sets and dark-stained escritoire, among other items. Is there anything I want to have, to move into my own home for keeps?

"Like what?" Is there a specific item he wants to liberate? I could help him sell it online if he wants to downsize a little.

By way of reply, he repairs to his room to fetch a certain crewneck sweater. I have seen this item before. It's dirt brown with a muddy, multicolored pattern. He picked it up from Marks & Spencer in the UK, who knows how long ago? At some point in the sweater's enduring life, it suffered an improper washing, thickening the wool and shrinking the sleeves. It also has a barrel shape about the torso. I know because he's made me try it on at least twice. This is quite possibly the least flattering garment I've ever put on my body, which is not even its worst quality—it's also scratchy and smells like a feral sheep. Every time I come here, he asks me to take it off his hands. He has no use for winterwear in Texas, he says, and it's still a good sweater. Every time, I accept it and promise that I will wear it with pride. As soon as I get my chance, I stow it in his guest-room closet where there is scarcely an extra hanger for all his backup dress shirts and eighties-vintage Adidas track pants. I fold the sweater carefully, stuffing it deep on the upper shelf behind the extra faux-silk bedspreads, knowing he'll resurrect it before too long. The next time I arrive he'll trot it out and foist it upon me all over again, just as he does with his fifty-year-old Doctor Zhivago lambskin coat that still hangs in the entranceway closet, releasing its funky must every time I open the door.

Before long, it becomes clear he means to give away any and all of his things, and that he wants me to have them, not just any someone. This generosity presents more than one problem. How would I get any of his heavier belongings to their destination when my address is over two thousand miles away? I've also amassed my own burden of clutter, endless books and seasonally used sporting gear, not all of which I like or want but nevertheless keep out of guilt and procrastination. "Whatever you want," he says, "I'll ship it to you."

The next day, during this daily transit through my work perch, he finds me editing student manuscripts. Every time he shuffles by, he drops some new tidbit of information, in his casually strategic way, as if it is freshly occurred to him. He prefaces this discussion by saying, "Now, don't get panicky."

"I'm not panicked," I say, my fingers hovered over the keyboard. "I'm right here."

During this visit, my dad wants to cover a certain kind of business. He wants to talk about the future and all his material affairs. We've been here before. But now my dad wants to discuss it with renewed enthusiasm, as if he'd saved it all up during the long months of our COVID separation.

He tells me that he never wants to move. His house is single-level—no stairs to negotiate save one step down in the garage to get to the car. He's had grab bars installed in his bathroom. The last thing he wants is a nursing home. The menu alone, with the pudding cups and the mystery-meat cutlets, would be hell for a man who appreciates napkins with thread counts. He has to take a road test soon, and he's a little worried about his eyesight. "If I can't drive, I'll take the Lyft." Until then, he's going to drive his Mercedes into the ground. I note that he's well on the way to doing that already.

I want to respect his wishes. That's what I tell him, even though I never expected to be the one appointed to the task of discussing them. I'm the last child I thought he'd choose for these conversations, especially when they sound like we're trying to find new paint colors for the walls or measurements for new curtains, which are incidentally also topics of interest to him these days. He's worried I'll consider it morbid, but I don't think he's going anywhere any time soon. I'm impressed by his resilience, by his bombproof genes, not to mention his amenable socioeconomic status and tight social connection to a chosen, party-going family. Luck follows him around like a faithful little dog. Sometimes I think he'll live forever, and I tell him so. "You've outlasted all your contemporaries," I say.

He swats at the air as he shuffles out of the room. "Let's not talk about that. It's depressing!"

Sometimes I think my dad would love nothing more than to live as the pampered old man in a customary multigenerational Indian household, nestled in the calm eye of a whirlwind of activity, cared for, worried about, fed, even nagged a little bit by a flock of relatives and descendants. But if that were true, many things would have unfolded differently in his past, and mine, too, since I have no children, by choice and circumstance, a development he's never asked me about, at least not directly. I can't really say I would have done things differently if I'd had the chance, and I don't think he would have, either. If the tape was rewound, I still can't imagine him as a person who'd submit to the sacrifices required of my grandfather's generation. Independence is his everything. It's also his conundrum since the freedom of bachelorhood is paid for in hours of solitude.

And yet, joy is currency with which the gifts of existence are repaid. Despite all that's befallen him throughout the years, he repeats this sentiment to me all the time. "You know," he says quite often, "life turned out pretty well."

DURING THIS VISIT, I drive my dad around to all his favorite places, spots where most of his friends insist on shaking my hand even though Texas is still seeing thousands of COVID cases a day. The sun's out. The birds are chirping. A hot breeze combs the trees. Everyone's sick of sickness, tired of being worried and afraid. This part of the world has decided to charge defiantly back into the barn burner of life, risks accepted, my dad very definitely included. Who am I to stop him?

My dad and I go out to eat almost every night at the usual place. He's grown a friendship with the restaurant owners, two close-knit families with long histories in the Rio Grande Valley. When he was in the hospital, many of them came to visit, carrying takeout boxes packed with his favorite soup. *He's like family,* they tell me almost every time I'm here.

But he has a family, I think. Or had one, anyway.

People come and go from the table. These are associates and acquaintances who've known him over the years. Sometimes they sit down at the empty chairs to order a drink and share a toast. "Larga vida!" they say as the glassware clinks.

"Larga vida!" my dad replies.

Some nights there's an endless river of friendly strangers shaking my hand or hugging my shoulders and kissing me on the cheek, and I can't say I mind all that much. "Your dad is a wonderful man," they say, over and over.

After a fair few of these good-natured encounters, once our solitude has been restored, my dad leans toward me to whisper in his conspiratorial way, "I have no idea who that was."

My dad, with his courtly manners, exudes refinement and wisdom, the idealized decency of a time gone by. He's also generous, funny, the best kind of troublemaker. He *is* a wonderful man in his own signature way. But I think so for reasons that are all my own, because I've known him in the best and worst of times.

During our moments of peak enmity, when our lives were too entangled, I couldn't get away from him fast enough. I only wanted what everybody wants, to be free. But that was also his greatest desire—and my mother's, too—to choose the shape of his own life and to accept the consequences even if it meant rejecting the fence-work of tradition or ripping up the prewritten script of his life. But there's an inbuilt reflexivity to the substance of liberty. If I demand freedom for myself, it's only fair to grant it in the opposite direction, reciprocally, to everyone else. That's the deal. So my dad lives as he pleases now, without me telling him what to do. Even though I was not around for many of his postdivorce renaissance years, I can see that he's become a different man, late in life, despite anyone's prognostications. In his own way, he's metamorphosed into a decent father. He remembers my birthday on occasion. He tells me he misses me when I'm at home in Canada. If too many days elapse between our long-distance calls, he blows up my voicemail with endearingly melodramatic guilt trips whose irony is not lost on me, all things considered. "Have you forgotten your old dad?"

Whenever I'm in Texas he reminds me all the time how much he likes having me around. He fusses over my well-being, even though it's hardly necessary at my age; I've made it this far caretaking my own material needs. Perhaps that's what enabled the relationship to resume. Neither one of us owes the other anything. Still, he tries to convince me I should have my flagging vision corrected with LASIK surgery, even if the idea of a robot shooting hot beams directly into my eyes makes me quaver. I can tell he worries about my pecuniary future—ironic for a big spender—his concern mitigated by the shielding presence of my spouse, whose masculine job it is to protect my security. Despite how his own marriage shook down, he's an Indian dad, through and through.

I tell him I've come to terms with the wobbliness of the artist's life, its patchwork of gains and losses. It's freeing to be a writer. Actually, it's pretty great—once you've had the inadvisable chat with your immigrant parents about your wide-eyed future failures. No one expects you to drive a Jag or pick up the tab or carry a Birkin bag. Besides, there's no life that's truly predictable, no story that progresses in a forever-upward curve. Despite anyone's bootstrap dreams, we're not much more than stardust and DNA, fertilized by the past and composted in the future. There's no getting out of this alive.

Whenever I look back on our family drama, I see it from a distance, according to the parallax of memory, with all its perceptual shifts and blind spots. The further back I travel, the slower objects appear to move, their prominence diminished. I suppose this is what it means to move on—not a feat of decision-making, but a kind of submission, a giving over, a letting go.

Despite the walks down memory lane, my dad can't stop giving away, either—belongings, dollar bills, even people— like a hose set to max flow. I've inherited but a whiff of this faith in unlimited abundance. I can't escape my mother's influence. When I visit her house, I find her in the old-growth forest of her material accumulations, beating it all back at the edges, sometimes capitulating to my offers to help with the purging. She's still a hardcore keeper, unable, by some precognitive guidance system, to really trust the future. And I can't say I do, either, not totally.

I think of fierce attachments, earthy and elemental, but also the missing links, the language I never learned, the food I attempt to replicate, the time I'll never make up for, the grandparents I never knew and the great-grands who came before them, the smells that take me back, the spices I can't find. It's the jokes I find funny. The way I tie my shoes and brush my teeth, the way I see through my eyes, a view of the world that belongs to me, but only partially. It belongs to others, too.

. . .

THERE IS A room in my dad's office that makes me shudder a little whenever I pass by. It's for storage, home to an impressive backlog of business paperwork, the accumulations of my dad's Texas medical career. Here he keeps file boxes piled five feet high and ten feet deep, an archive edited about as much as his shirt collection over the decades, which is to say never pruned at all. Now that my dad's office space is on the realtor's block, all of this, among many other objects and belongings, must be dealt with in an appropriate, professional manner. Every single sheet and form in this room requires destruction. Easy enough, I think. Remove a few bulldog clips here and there, and off they go to Iron Mountain.

The wallpaper in the storage room is white with a feathery pink and gray-blue texture. I know it all too well because during this visit, I spend many hours, days in fact, staring at the pattern. In the storage room, I come to ask if an entire forest has been felled in the making of all this copier paper, nixing whatever offsets I generated in my long career as a tree-planter. There are hundreds of boxes containing hundreds of file folders, some of them nested doubly and triply. And, alas, in each and every folder I discover two metal prong fasteners, affixed with tenacious glue. After a heartbreaking trip to the shredding facility, I confirm the unfortunate fact that they must all come out, zillions of them. The metal prongs won't make it through the shredder teeth without destroying the machinery.

I rip out one of these devil's hairpins and hold it up to my dad for examination. "Whose idea was this?" I ask. Who made this decision all those years ago?

My dad blames it on Frances, the office manager. Frances blames it on my dad. As much as I want to believe my own dear father, I know his habits well. They sometimes make me wonder if there's a word for his natural way of doing things: byzantine layers of unnecessary complexity resulting in maximum future inconvenience.

And so we do what needs to be done, Frances and me. We tear out all the offending metal. At first it's just repetitive drudgery, countless folders and armloads of paper, the office filled with the rhythmic sounds of ripping. But after a hundred tiny cuts on my hands and hours of stacking files like cordwood, I begin to see the shape of my dad's career, each box a trip back in time as we move from the front of the room to the boxes buried in the back. My hands brush over all those missing years.

At the back of the pile I find a box, crushed beneath the weight of the ones above, holding a random assortment of my dad's personal paperwork, as if it were junk tossed there in a moment of haste, or miscellany never unpacked after a move. I unearth a manila envelope stuffed with his old photocopied CVs showing the details of all his fellowships and residencies and board certifications. I find a photo album containing long-forgotten photos of us, his kids, during childhood. Many are of my sister in her teenage years and some are of my brother and me at our high school graduation, an event my dad didn't attend. There are quite a few of him in his natural habitat, at a birthday party, I can tell from the cake, that some unremembered friend once threw for him. He's wearing a tux. He's air-kissing a white woman with big hair.

At the very bottom, there's a sheaf of documents with sky-blue covers, all the legal volleys sent by my mother's lawyers over the years, the paper trail of divorce. I never tell my dad about these, destined as they were for the shredders anyway, or a next life as recycled paper towels. But when the time comes, I'll carry the transcript of *Gill v. Gill* home in my suitcase. I'll call my mother to ask for her blessing to excavate—something, in the end, I never get around to doing.

"Go ahead," she'll say with a sigh that could tip over at any second into a kind of weary laughter. She'll summarize for me the long litigious process, but I've heard that story many times over already and certainly know the outcome. She's decades past these old battles. What would be the point of revisiting? If it takes seven years for the body to renew all its cells, then we've recycled ourselves at least a few times over. We've spent more years apart than we ever did together. Life has moved on for all of us, mostly for the better.

After I'm done for the day at my dad's office, I carry an armload of his paperwork and the old photo albums back to his house. When I sit down on the sofa beside him to present these artifacts, he goes straight for the snapshots, flipping the album pages, remembering his friends to me, assembling the loose photos in a little pile on the coffee table. Then we proceed backward through his CVs as if we're engaged in a very small archaeological dig complete with anecdotes and quips for each layer of the journey. "Don't you want to keep some of these things?" I ask.

"What for?" he wants to know. He's never been a memorabilia person. The past is the past.

In the back pages of the photo album, we find an envelope sent through the mail by my mother containing my first-year undergrad transcripts. My dad and I read over the codes for courses I scarcely remember taking along with my unexceptional assortment of A-minuses and B-plusses. There's a note in the corner, a cheery little jotting in my mother's handwriting that reads: *What a kid!*

"Look at that," he says, as if these marks were freshly received, as if I am enrolled in an undergraduate odyssey right now, not decades ago. "You did a good job."

AFTER TWO WEEKS in McAllen, it's time for me to go home, whatever home means to our clan in any given moment. My dad and I go out to dinner one last time, but just like usual, he gets the better of me when it comes to late-night endurance. Yet another slab of meat and a salad, and then I announce it's my bedtime if I want to get up early enough for my flight. He flips me the keys and tells me he'll get a ride home with Arturo, a friend of his who's just dropped by for a cigar.

Early the next morning, I stagger out of the guest room while rubbing my eyes and find him before the TV with all the lights on, looking alert and refreshed, as if he'd gone to bed at an age-appropriate hour. We're back where we started. I ask him what time he got home.

"Not until two o'clock," he tells me with a little chuckle. He blames it on his friends, more of whom came by to carouse. By the time he returned, he says, it made more sense just to stay up until my alarm went off. He's wearing a new outfit, I notice, a light sweater over his dinner shirt.

He drives me to the airport. It's five A.M. and still dark out. It rained overnight, and my dad plows up to the green lights, crashing through all the puddles, while I stomp my imaginary brake pedal. He tells me again how much he's going to miss me. He takes me to the drop-off zone, puts the car in park but leaves it running—the stop, drop, and roll technique of airport deposit that my family has used for many years. He gets out with his trusty double-leg swing as I haul my luggage from the trunk. Then he gives me a sideways almost-hug, the most enthusiastic one yet, complete with a few solid back pats.

He waves goodbye, and I wave goodbye. I wheel my little suitcase away. He calls out to request that I text him at boarding so he can safely go to bed.

"Absolutely," I say.

Then he hails me again. I should text him when I finally get home so he knows I made it back in one piece. Then he asks me to say hello to my husband on his behalf.

"I will," I shout back over the din of taxis and gliding cars. I take a few more steps, the space between us expanding and thinning all at once.

Then he calls out one final time. "When will you be back?"

"In a few months," I say. There it is, the damn twinge in the throat, but I pull myself away and turn toward the sliding glass doors.

"See you," he says.

"Next time!" I reply.

He's not usually one for looking back, and neither am I when it comes to goodbyes. But these days I remind myself to take those extra glances, to burn them into memory, just in case, just to hold me over while our lives peel apart again. Then my dad goes around to the driver's side and gets back in behind the wheel. In another minute, he's gliding away into the velvety heat and the morning darkness, facing ahead, both hands on the wheel. Back at home he'll fall asleep with the TV blaring then wake up at midday to resume his genuflections to the gods of contentment, until we meet again.

See you next time. That's what I always say.

Larga vida!

Larga vida!

Long life, long life.

ACKNOWLEDGMENTS

THIS STORY WAS WRITTEN IN QATHET, WITHIN THE ancestral territory of the Tla'amin Nation, where I live as a guest.

Thanks to the Canada Council for the Arts and the Access Copyright Foundation, whose granting program supported the research during a time of widespread library closures. I owe a debt to Nell Irvin Painter, Jayne O. Ifekwunigwe, Chamion Caballero, Peter Aspinall, and many other historians and scholars in the fields of postcolonial and mixed-race studies whose work informed this project. Also to Khushwant Singh, J. S. Grewal, and Yasmin Khan— their authoritative histories of the Sikhs, India, and Partition were essential reading.

Haley Cullingham and Jordan Ginsberg at *Hazlitt* published a feature article that got this whole thing started. Jessica McDiarmid, who fact-checked this book, for her impeccable skills. Taylor McGowan is owed thanks and apologies for my abuse of the Oxford comma. Yang Kim and Kate Sinclair for their beautiful cover designs in the United States and Canada. My agent, Samantha Haywood, for moving mountains and for her steady companionship through thick and thin. Nicole Winstanley at Penguin Random House Canada and Aubrey Martinson at Crown did more for me behind the scenes than I'll ever know. Deborah Sun de la Cruz and Madhulika Sikka were the editors of my dreams, and without their thoughtful guidance I'd probably still be wandering in the forest.

My excellent friend Nola Poirier beta-tested this work under my totally unreasonable conditions. Megan Cole and Zsuzsi Gartner remind me that it's no fun to be a writer all alone. Jaswinder Legha connected me to some of the best family lore. KT, as always, who reads every page and makes me laugh with unfailing regularity. I'm grateful for the love and support of my family, in all their many shades.

ABOUT THE AUTHOR

CHARLOTTE GILL is a bestselling and award-winning writer of fiction and narrative nonfiction. *Ladykiller,* her first book, was the recipient of the Danuta Gleed Literary Award for short fiction. *Eating Dirt,* a tree-planting memoir, was a #1 national bestseller in Canada. Her work has appeared in *Vogue* and *Hazlitt.* Gill teaches writing in the MFA program in creative nonfiction at the University of King's College and is the Rogers Communications Chair of Literary Journalism at the Banff Centre for Arts and Creativity. She lives in British Columbia, Canada.

charlottegill.com

ABOUT THE TYPE

This book was set in Sabon, a typeface designed by the well-known German typographer Jan Tschichold (1902–74). Sabon's design is based upon the original letter forms of sixteenth-century French type designer Claude Garamond and was created specifically to be used for three sources: foundry type for hand composition, Linotype, and Monotype. Tschichold named his typeface for the famous Frankfurt typefounder Jacques Sabon (c. 1520–80).